Advance Praise for *Real You Incorporated*

"Kaira Rouda has been shaking up everyone's idea about how to have a real and differentiated "brand" in the world of real estate for awhile. She's the real deal, and in this book she shares a simple process to understand, develop, and express the real you in your own brand, company, and environment. This book provides the fundamentals of branding creation and execution with an approach that is uniquely Kaira—fresh, straight forward, and fun."

Anne Randolph, Publisher of *LORE* magazine

"From surviving snark-infested waters, culture vultures, and passion poppers who attempt to undermine both you and your business, Rouda's systematic approach for female entrepreneurs provides you with the essentials you need to create a business that makes both your heart and your wallet sing."

Bernice L. Ross, CEO of www.RealEstateCoach.com, nationally syndicated real estate columnist, and author of *Waging War on Real Estate's Discounters*

"*Real You Incorporated* will not only educate women entrepreneurs about the essentials of branding and marketing, but will help them voice their inner compass—that intuition that guides them as they navigate the overwhelming number of decisions they must make as business owners. Rouda reminds readers to stay true to themselves, and she teaches them how to translate their personal convictions and passions into elements of a successful business."

Ginny Wilmerding, small business consultant and author of *Smart Women and Small Business: How to Make the Leap from Corporate Careers to the Right Small Enterprise*

"Kaira has always provided a fresh, unique perspective for entrepreneurs—her insights surrounding women in business in particular are unparalleled. This book embodies both Kaira's enthusiasm and business acumen, and will serve as an invaluable resource for savvy women across the nation."

John E. Featherston, President and CEO of RISMedia, publisher of *Real Estate* magazine

"*Real You Incorporated* is a gift to those who open its pages. Part inspiration, part how-to manual, part life invitation, it is imminently readable and is a joy-filled call to redefining ourselves. It is thrilling to read something that is so grounded and simultaneously so affirming!"

Cynthia Lazarus, CEO/President of YWCA-Columbus

"*Real You Incorporated* is a toolkit of inspiration and limit-exploding exercises, created by a real visionary who knows what it takes for women entrepreneurs to grow their baby businesses into strong brands and profitable enterprises."

Tara-Nicholle Nelson, Founder & chief visionary of REThinkRealEstate.com, and author of *The Savvy Woman's Homebuying Handbook*

"What a fantastic book. This book is exactly what I needed . . . there are so many basic life rules that I have tried to live by for a long time in spite of those "snarks." *Real You Incorporated* offers great advice for anyone starting a journey into the business world."

Rita Wolfe, Corporate Director of Civic Affairs, Dispatch Printing Company

"*Real You Incorporated* gives real insight and real advice to those looking to start their own business."

Ja-Naé Duane, President/Founder of Wild Women Entrepreneurs

Real You
Incorporated

8 Essentials For Women Entrepreneurs

Kaira Sturdivant Rouda

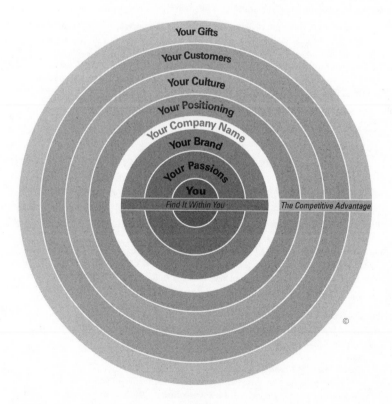

WILEY

John Wiley & Sons, Inc.

Published by John Wiley & Sons, Inc., Hoboken, New Jersey.
Published simultaneously in Canada.

For general information on our other products and services or for technical
support, please contact our Customer Care Department within the United States at
(800) 762-2974, outside the United States at (317) 572-3993, or fax (317) 572-4002.

Designations used by companies to distinguish their products are often claimed by
trademarks. In all instances where the author or publisher is aware of a claim, the product
names appear in Initial Capital letters. Readers, however, should contact the appropriate
companies for more complete information regarding trademarks and registration.

Wiley also publishes its books in a variety of electronic formats. Some content that
appears in print may not be available in electronic books. For more information about
Wiley products, visit our web site at www.wiley.com.

Library of Congress Cataloging-in-Publication Data

Rouda, Kaira Sturdivant, 1963-
    Real you incorporated : 8 essential rules for women entrepreneurs / Kaira
Sturdivant Rouda.
        p. cm.
    ISBN 978-0-470-17658-0 (cloth)
        1. Women-owned business enterprises.   2. Minority business enterprises.
3. New business enterprises.   4. Businesswomen.   5. Entrepreneurship.   I. Title.
HD2358.R68 2008
658'.041082—dc22

                                                                2007050502

Printed in the United States of America
10   9   8   7   6   5   4   3   2   1

To my grandmothers, who were pioneers each in her own way;
To my parents, who taught me a woman can do anything;
To my sister, who taught me to fight back;
And to my brother, who is always on my side;
To my husband, who stands beside me every day;
To my boys, who are already entrepreneurs;
And to my daughter, who will ride the third wave to her dreams.

Contents

Introduction

Every 60 seconds, a woman starts a business, according to The White House Project. Sound big? It is, and there's a lot of buzz going on about it. And it's changing the way the world works. I speak frequently to organizations, real estate or otherwise, and every time I make a speech, the number one question I am asked is: "How do I do it all?"

This question doesn't refer to buying a billboard or a banner ad. It means, "How do I position my company? Differentiate it? Win?" It also means, "How do I manage four kids *and* a business?" The answer is being real—personally and through your company, and creating a culture that fits you and your dreams. This answer is why I wrote this book.

So, what does it mean to be real? It means your values—and your personality—are in sync with your business's operations and its people. *Real You Incorporated* is for women business owners or those who are considering becoming one. Read it before you launch your business, before your first or next hire, and before you find your first, or next, advertising agency. *Real You Incorporated* teaches you that your brand isn't just what consumers see—it's also what they don't see. Branding isn't just advertising or public relations. It's identity. It's about you, the culture of your organization, and more.

At my company—Real Living, one of the nation's fastest-growing residential real estate firms, founded in 2002—we were into real branding long before *Real Simple* and Dr. Phil. These brands know women are their audience and are in tune with our collective need to find real meaning in our personal and professional lives.

A key message in *Real You Incorporated* is that women have clout—lots of it—and are gaining more every day. We rock in business. We are world-class consumers. Consider these facts:

♦ One out of every 11 adult women is an entrepreneur, says the Institute for the Study of Educational Entrepreneurship.

♦ Women are starting businesses at twice the rate of men, employing one of every seven workers in the United States, and the majority of women-owned businesses continue to grow about two times faster than other firms, according to the Center for Women's Business Research.

♦ American women make up the *largest national economy on earth*—we are 51 percent of the population, but we buy 85 percent of *everything,* according to *USA Today*.

Most business and marketing books talk to women about how to fit into and play the games of the predominantly male business world. Many teach how to network or how to infuse real emotion into the workplace. Others focus on the work-life and family-life overlap. These aren't secrets to women.

Women need to acknowledge their collective power and the fact that we are making the rules. We want a workplace that is authentic (real!), family-friendly, and rewarding. We want to communicate these values to our employees and customers. We know we aren't there yet. We've been trying to be part of the boys' club for too long, reading books about the same. It's time to change.

How do you get to where you want to go? *Real You Incorporated* contains eight Real Facts (or chapters) to help you. In each Real Fact of *Real You Incorporated,* you'll also find three life lessons followed by real stories—profiles of successful women entrepreneurs—and three action steps and questions.

An added element of each Real Fact is the opportunity to create your Real You Incorporated chart (a.k.a. RYI chart), a visual reminder of the process you're embarking on. By the end of the book, you will have created your own unique representation of you and your real brand.

Ready? Let's go! It's time for real women to create real brands.

SECTION I

❊ ❊ ❊

Find It Within You

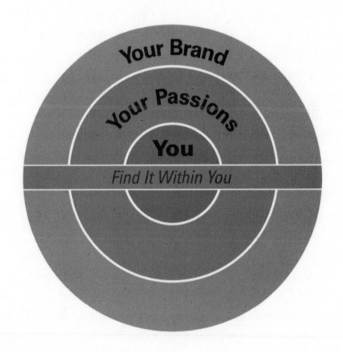

You are unique. But you knew that. Did you also know you are uniquely marketable? You just need to learn how to express your unique personal brand as a Real marketable business brand. Unabashedly. Powerfully. You can do it. As a woman entrepreneur, you occupy a special position. If you can capture your essence, and express it through everything you do in your personal and business life, you will bring a richer, more sincere, and sustainable message to the business community.

That's the premise of the first three Real Facts of *Real You Incorporated*. Once you can discover and love your personal brand, you can launch it as a real brand, one that is powerful and different from a man's. The process for bringing the true you to the surface is one we'll cover in the first section of the book. We'll unlock the true you. Your passions. Your personal brand essence. Why? Because these qualities and values, loves, and desires aren't distinct from you as a businesswoman, even though traditional corporate business customs and protocol teach the opposite. For generations, businesswomen have been forced to fit in. Eliminate their feminine traits. Act like a man to get ahead. That's not real. And it's not sustainable without a lot of personal angst.

After reading Section One, you'll be able to articulate your personal brand. Clearly. Proudly. You bring a unique perspective to the world. It needs to be shared fully, not compromised by traditions and structures outside of you. Once you've found it within, and documented it on your chart, you can take steps to create the world you want to work in. The second section will explain how to leverage your competitive advantage.

With *Real You Incorporated,* you are doing more than reading a book. You are creating a tangible vision of your personal and business world—and how they come together in a powerful, unique way. If you're an entrepreneur already, documenting the Real You throughout the first section of this chart will prove to be an invaluable experience. If you're just getting started on realizing your dreams, the RYI chart will provide a road map for you and your new business. Display it proudly; refer to it often. Many women find the central core of their chart remains the same over time—you, your passions, and your brand essence. What may shift is the business expression of your brand. If you sell your company, merge with another, or start an entirely new business, your competitive advantage layers will change a bit.

But the *you* at the heart of it all will remain the same. Understanding your personal brand—embracing it—and your personal power are the focal points of this section. Here, you will complete the first three circles of the RYI chart: you, your passions, your brand essence. Let's get started.

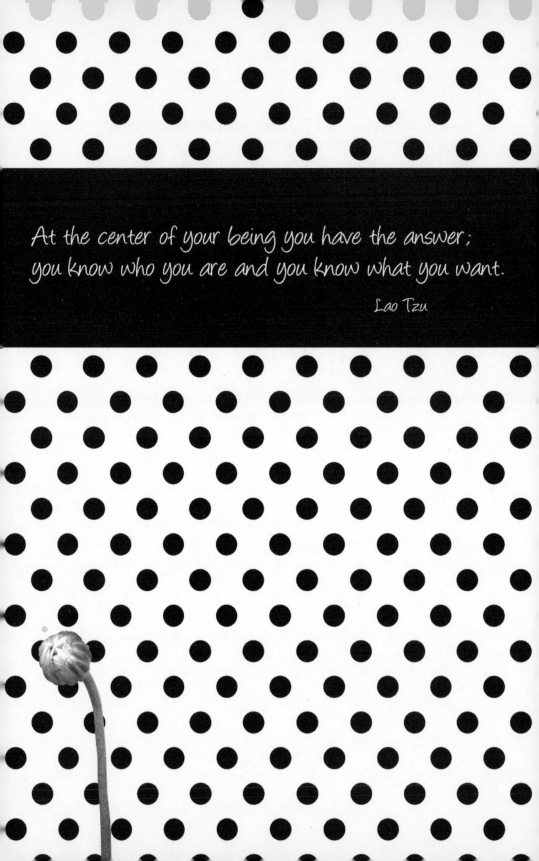

At the center of your being you have the answer;
you know who you are and you know what you want.

Lao Tzu

It All Starts With You

It all starts with you—and your dreams. That's what got you thinking about owning your own business in the first place. Like me, you want to do it right. You want to make a difference. You want to call the shots. And we're not alone. Women are starting their own businesses at twice the rate of men, leaving corporate jobs because of inflexibility, frustration with the good old boys' club and the glass ceiling, lack of creativity in the workplace, and pure boredom. And many young women aren't even entering the corporate world at all, choosing to embrace their inner entrepreneur from the get-go.

To discover the true entrepreneur in you, it's all about being real.

> *Real* (r ' l) adj., being or occurring in fact or actuality; having verifiable existence. Hence the name of the book, *Real You Incorporated*.

It means to be genuine, truthful, and authentic with nothing fake or contrived in everything you do from creating your positioning statement to hiring employees to help you realize your dream.

Real You Incorporated is a book about empowering women in business, specifically women entrepreneurs. If you're one of these women, kudos. But if you're still an executive working for someone else, *Real You Incorporated* can help strengthen your personal brand, crucial in today's business world. Because once you discover and love your personal brand, you can bring your business to the market as a real brand, one that is powerful and distinct from a man's. Within these pages, you'll find some business self-help advice, a bit of work-life balance sharing, and naturally, a little memoir to set the stage. But predominantly, this is a book about women and celebrating their natural entrepreneurial bent.

After reading *Real You Incorporated,* you will better understand your personal brand and be able to deliver a more sincere, sustainable, and richer business concept to the world. Keep in mind that interconnectivity and integration are the key notions today. You are a brand. The company you create is a brand. When the essence of each—you and your business—are in alignment, you create a real brand.

In this Real Fact, you'll begin to create your RYI chart. You'll fill in the first layer of the circle as you work through this fact: It all starts with you. As you work your way through the book, you will begin to create a unique, customized visualization of your business. Along the way, I'll provide personal examples as illumination, and I'll enlist the help of some real entrepreneurial women to share their experiences, too.

In this Real Fact, you learn about the following:

♦ Your future starts now

♦ Learn from your past

♦ Describe yourself in one word

Life Lesson One: Your future starts now

And it's okay to grab it. The premise of *Real You Incorporated* is that you, as a businessperson and a woman, want an authentic, transparent, dynamic, relevant, and real brand. Both personally and for the company you are creating. You want and deserve the right to follow your dreams in a uniquely feminine way with enthusiastic pursuit. Women do have more choices than ever before. The problem today is: What choice is right? For you—not for your neighbor, your co-worker, your spouse, or your mom. For you. And I'm not talking about an unbalanced approach to your business goals. Nope, that can be risky. As with anything else in life, the time can come when you turn around and realize a single-minded focus on your career can feel a lot like being a one-dimensional person. Not good. Not interesting. Not fulfilling.

The key to having a rewarding business is having one that speaks to your inner strengths, bolsters your passions, and engages your heart. That doesn't mean you need to default to a traditionally feminine career, although those careers are right for some. It simply means that you follow your instincts and your intellect, use all of your skills, and do it in a uniquely you way. All the while realizing there still aren't a lot of road maps.

It takes a combination of instinct, experience, and confidence to build a real brand. It takes the same to build a real life. It's not without constant redefinition and integration, both of the people around us, and ourselves. As a 40-something woman, I find myself looking in the mirror and realizing with no uncertainty that I will continue to redefine my life, my brand, and my work. It won't be like my mother's (just as I constantly joke that this book won't be like one written by my father), and it won't be like yours. But if my company plays to my true self, encompasses my passions, fuels my need for power, rings true to my customers, allows me the flexibility to share my gifts with the community and be there for my husband and kids, I'm happy, and always growing.

It's not about having it all; it's about having what you want. And it's never really been about a work-life balance. It's more about integrating work and family with your personal goals. It starts with knowing yourself and your definition of fulfillment. Next, you need to funnel your natural and sparkling ambition into creating a business that makes your heart sing. And, let's not forget, makes your wallet heavier. Women are notorious for not leveraging their worth in business, not asking for, or worse, minimizing their value. Real brands don't do that because they have confidence in their worth. Your real company can and should have monetary value to you, as well as personal meaning, all the while allowing you to integrate the people in life who are important to you.

It's never too early or too late to create your own personal real brand. You can start the building blocks right now, in whatever stage of your career you find yourself. Your life, up to this point, has helped you plot a course toward entrepreneurship, even if you didn't know that! And if you're already an entrepreneur, begin now with *Real You Incorporated* to reinvigorate your existing company by following these life lessons and action steps, and by learning from the real stories of successful women entrepreneurs.

What does it mean to be real? It means your values and your personality are in sync with your business operations and its people. It means you surround yourself with people who think and act like you—true believers—inside and outside of the workplace. It means you nurture your passion with a network of mentors, friends, and activities. It also means you reach out and give back— empowering other women, just like you've been empowered.

At the heart of it, a real brand is about creating the business and life you want by designing a conscious culture of your choosing. If you're in business, you have a culture and an identity. *Real You Incorporated* will help you define and refine it.

Women are pulled in multiple directions. Before you can build your personal brand and company, you need focus. Step back, put aside the demands in your life, clear the mind clutter and take time to focus on you, your goals, where you're going, and where you want your business plan to go. Get in touch with your feelings, so you can act on them. Get a pencil and paper or have your computer handy, so you can write or type your thoughts. Be prepared to record them for reflection now and later.

Make time for yourself, because your future starts now.

To get your creative juices flowing, envision a blank canvas in front of you. There are no directions or guidelines, just wide open spaces.

QUESTIONS TO THINK ABOUT

1. What does being real mean to you? What could you do to be more true, genuine, authentic?

2. Are you real? In your everyday life, at work, at home, or do you change personalities and play different roles in different settings?

3. Can you allow yourself some time to think, plan, and dream?

ACTION STEPS

1. Take time to get organized. You will be filling out the RYI chart, but you'll also be bubbling up some ideas you'll want to record.

2. Take a break. If you can, head to the hills, the ocean, or just a hotel for a night or a weekend, by yourself. This is tough, especially if you're a parent. But you are allowed to have some guilt-free alone time. It's vital.

3. Allow yourself to think big, be ambitious. This is your life, so get it right.

A Real Story

Marilyn Marr

Meet Marilyn Marr, born in 1951, communications
firm owner, M&R Management Communication, LLC.
Business owner since 1995.

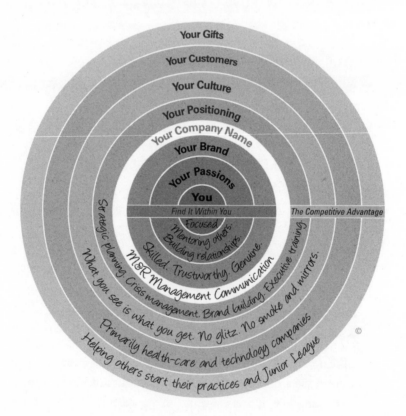

I started my public relations counsel practice in 1995 (age 44) after 23 years in public relations. Actually, the practice was meant to be a stopgap—a way for me to cover my share of the household expenses while I earned my gemology certification (primarily through home study courses) from the Gemological Institute of America. My plan was to establish a custom jewelry business. But as soon as I left, I started getting calls from people I'd worked with over the years. After a short while, I realized it wasn't a new career I needed, but a new environment. That's when I knew my future was about to begin.

Without even sending out an "I'm open for business" letter, my workload took off. I got so busy, I never got around to completing the gemology coursework. Being real for me meant trying something new. I never saw myself as the work-by-yourself, entrepreneurial type, but when I headed down that path, I realized it was one of the best things I'd ever done. The lesson here is that sometimes where you're supposed to be or to venture isn't always obvious. I enjoy the flexibility (such that it is) and being responsible only for myself, rather than a staff. About three months after starting my practice, I had an ah-ha moment. It suddenly dawned on me that the reason I felt so unusually calm—even though I had no guaranteed paycheck—was that for the first time in years, I was not trying to figure out what I wanted to do with my career. My future was clear, and that was a great feeling.

Marilyn's future started the moment she took a chance on herself. At the time, she thought she needed a new career, but what she discovered was the joy of being her own boss in a profession she loved. Marilyn's story demonstrates how ah-ha moments reflect light on the real you waiting to become. Becoming real, true to yourself, is a process, and it's never too late to start.

♦ If you haven't read it for a while, or ever, pick up a copy of *Gift from the Sea* by Anne Morrow Lindbergh. Since 1955, when it was originally printed, the quiet and reflective prose of this remarkable woman allows you to contemplate your own definition of happiness and creativity. Relax with it as you realize the future is now.

Life Lesson Two: Learn from your past

As I mentioned earlier, there's no perfect time to create your own personal brand. It can happen at any point during your career. Up until this time in your life and from here on out, you have been building your identity. And, as we all know in life, you gain strength through adversity. All of your past experiences—good, bad, and ugly—along with the people you've chosen to love and befriend, have made you who you are today.

It's vitally important for you to have an accurate view of yourself—you cannot brand yourself correctly without it. And while there are any number of self-help experts, books, and the like to help you get to know yourself, you can do it on your own.

> Your history—with all of its highs and lows—is part of your essence.

Your prejudices come from inside. Your likes and dislikes. Your management style and so much more. It's time to reflect. As I look back, my life today is a true reflection of and reaction to my past— and the basis for who I am.

Lucky for me, I was raised to believe women could do anything. My father, a marketing professor and author, who later became a high-profile business consultant, encouraged me to aim high and be my own boss. My mother had a huge influence, too. They held themselves to high standards and raised the bar high for my siblings and me, too. I had a very traditional 1950s upbringing in the heart of the 1970s. I was raised by a father who was the first in his family to graduate from college—who went on to earn a Ph.D.—and a mother who moved from her parents' house, where she lived during college, to her first home with my dad. Together, they created the American dream they were taught to find.

My drive and ambition came from my overachieving father, and my mom, whose home was run more efficiently than any corporation. She was every bit as accomplished as my father, just in a different setting. When I think of my mom, my memories growing up are full of perfectly prepared and artfully presented meals. Immaculate gardens. Room parents and PTO. Crafts. And a sparkling home, all part of a full and privileged life of country clubs and tennis matches in the suburbs. And while I ended up creating a family literally five miles away in the exact same suburb, my interpretation is wholly different from hers. Not better or worse, just absolutely different, yet certainly a reflection of her. I took all of her attributes—commitment, dedication, and perseverance—and applied them to a life that is real for me, one full of home and career.

With an English degree from Vanderbilt University under my belt, I began pursuing a writing job.

In my first full-time job after college, I worked as a reporter and started what turned out to be a popular column covering the advertising and communications industry. It was a chance to combine two passions—writing and marketing—and to rub shoulders with agency principals. I wrote about their campaigns and attended memorable martini luncheons while learning journalism and a bit about advertising at the same time.

When the behavior of my editor made the newsroom unbearable, a co-worker and I approached the publisher. She told me I should move on, and so I did. I had learned a lot in my first job. Unfortunately, there would be many more bad boss stories in my future. But with each one of them, I learned a little more about myself and about what I would strive to create when I started my own company. At my first advertising agency job, one of the principals stood at the door every morning, exuding every bit the pompous character he was, to make sure everyone arrived on time properly dressed (which meant to him skirts only). Meanwhile, a photo of his bikini-clad secretary adorned his desk. I was making the best of a bad situation when one of the account managers, my boss, left to join another, bigger firm in town. I had nothing to do with the move, yet I was fired between Christmas and New Year's Eve. I was told my work, which up until that time had been great, was unsatisfactory.

> When the unexpected happens, don't panic. Every set-back is an opportunity to open another door, discover another path.

Keep your eyes open for them. And, remember, you learn more from bad experiences than good ones. In my case, one bad boss experience led to an interview and then a sales job at an urban contemporary radio station. I'll never forget the incredulous look the sales manager, Bill Brooks, gave me during my interview. He showed me a stack of resumes of people who had tons more sales experience, but I persuaded him to take a chance on me. I was able to translate my status as the only Caucasian and woman on the sales team to success by landing major mainstream advertising accounts for the station. Little did I know—yes, every setback is an opportunity—that radio is the perfect venue for learning the ins and outs of advertising, and commission sales is a great way to toughen up.

So don't be afraid to walk away when the going gets tough, and remember to breathe if experiences don't work out the way you planned. I never would have met Bill if the newspaper job hadn't become unbearable. And I wouldn't have tested the safety net of my first job. I bet you have similar stories.

As you're moving forward with your entrepreneurial dreams, remember it's important to take a look back. Learn from your past. It's chock-full of important information. Pursue your dreams head-on with stealth determination, but be prepared to shift gears at any moment, sometimes quickly.

Writing my history for this book really helped me to crystallize the key work experiences in my life, the ones that made me who I am today. Yours have, too. The good, the bad, and the really bad. Taken together, they are your history and the source of your reactions to events taking place today. If you wonder about certain idiosyncrasies and behaviors you default to, check your rearview mirror for the answer. It's there. Now think about the questions that follow and complete the action steps.

QUESTIONS TO THINK ABOUT

1. Remember a formative setback you've had, personally or professionally. How can you use the memory of this experience as you build your plan for the future?

2. What are your greatest professional accomplishments to date? Start by thinking about your first job and your very first boss. What's a takeaway?

3. Reflect upon the feelings associated with these experiences from your past. Commit them to memory and keep them handy as reminders of how strong *you* have become.

ACTION STEPS

1. Create a list of characteristics you find positive about previous work experiences. Next, list the negative attributes. What are your most resilient attributes—flexibility, determination, confidence? These are important, too. If you aren't a writer, that's okay. Get someone to help you. That's a lesson you'll learn later in the book: Don't be afraid to ask for help when you need it.

2. Write your life story. With every experience, you grow. What have you learned from all of the jobs in your past? If you're like me, you've had too many to write about each one in depth. The key is to remember what aspect of each job or career helped make you who you are today. Control and edit yourself by limiting the length to two pages, 500 words max. This doesn't have to be manuscript quality. It's for your use. Again, if you aren't a writer and are struggling to get it down, ask for help.

3. Take the information you've generated here and condense it. If you can, create a short, one paragraph version. You in a snap shot. There is no getting out of this one. It's your resume, in paragraph form. You can do this.

A Real Story

Connie Spruill

Meet Connie Spruill, born in 1950, president and owner of Attitude Marketers International, Inc., a people and business development company. Business owner since 1983.

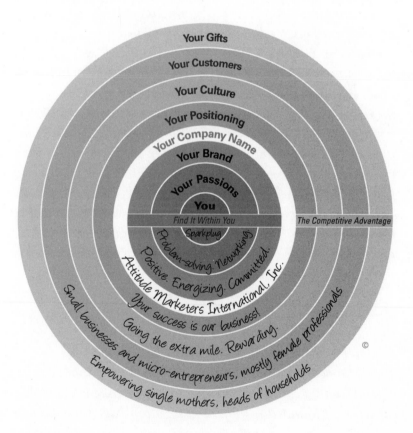

In 1976, before I started my first business in 1978, I worked briefly for a lumber wholesale broker. The third generation had just taken over ownership, and I was the secretary who held down the fort while the young boss spent time on the golf course and doing other extracurricular activities. Even though I was going through a divorce and had two small children, for 18 months I had a chance to learn the lumber wholesale company from the ground up. When a spot opened up for a senior salesperson within the company, of course I applied for it. I didn't get it. They hired some jock who sat around and listened to ball games on his radio and didn't know the difference between a stick of wood and a stick of celery. When I approached my boss to ask why I didn't qualify for this position, his answer was like a slap in the face. He said: "He has a family to support." The guy was 23 years old, married, and his wife was pregnant. I guess my two daughters were seen as pups instead of human beings, and my sales were accidents. At the end of the year, the new and experienced salesperson got the bonus I thought I deserved, and I got a $20 necklace. Well, three weeks later, I was in my own office (thanks to the help of a friend), wholesaling lumber to all the customers that I dealt with at the other business. My customers stayed loyal to me. A year later, the old company went out of business.

What did I learn? I control my destiny. I didn't have to know everything about the business or industry, I just had to know people who did and form an alliance. If I can learn how to bid for million-dollar construction supply jobs and get them shipped to job sites on time and do it all without a bank line of credit, I can do anything. During the time I was in construction, I founded a trade organization called the Association of Business and Professional Women in Construction. I discovered that I enjoyed training and mentoring other women to follow in my path and become business owners, especially in male-dominated industries. I launched my next company, Attitude Marketers International, in 1983 to do just that.

I think entrepreneurs are a unique type. Many of us morph our services according to our need for a new challenge. My brand has always centered on my expertise to satisfy needs of professional women, women business owners, and those who seek to be either. I can sell feng shui, business development expertise, and counsel in career transitions and financial life planning for all phases of a woman's life. I have not done all of these things at the same time, but as my female market changes, I change my service and products to meet the need. This includes obtaining any licensing, education, and credentias to satisfy the need. Through all of my work experiences and life experiences, I've learned. But my personal brand stays the same. It's me. A really savvy entrepreneurial woman will know this. The target market won't care how many things you have been involved in, only that you take care of them as they move along. Keep your personal brand visible. Learn from your past, and help it to propel your future.

If you sat down with Connie and talked to her about her life and her many challenges—including the strength to leave an abusive husband even though it meant homelessness, raising two small daughters on her own, and eventually becoming a successful entrepreneur—you would find a woman who not only learned from her past, but grew stronger with each bad experience. Her story is a perfect example of facing negative life experiences and growing stronger and more powerful because of them.

♦ *The Feminine Mystique* by Betty Friedan is a must-read. Talk about a look into the past that will remind you of how far we've come, and how far we still have to go. It's a classic, and so are you, no matter your age.

Life Lesson Three: Describe yourself in one word

Now that I've shared a couple of my important life lessons and you've read a couple of real stories from other women, it's time to shift the focus to you. As I said at the beginning of this Real Fact, building a business begins with you. And, please remember, you are the creator of your business, but you are always a distinct essence apart from it, too. It doesn't matter whether you're creating a sole proprietorship or a huge enterprise with lots of employees. You want to be the heart of it, but it's not the same as you. The first layer of the RYI chart is the one word you will use to sum up yourself. Just one. That's it. Can you describe yourself in a word?

Get started with a simple exercise, which we'll revisit and enlarge as you move through the book. Follow the example presented at the beginning of the Real Fact.

Make a circle, with the word *you* in the middle, and begin the search for the one word that defines you.

The one word you can replace the word *you* with. Think of it as zeroing in on your essence. Think about yourself in the past and where you are now, and blend them together. It's difficult, but it's essential. Remember this is a process. And not everyone sees you in the same light. If it helps, capture the essence that also relates to your work style. After all, we are starting a business here. Here are some steps to help you.

QUESTIONS TO THINK ABOUT

1. Have you ever had a nickname? There are truths to be found there. Mine was spaz, by the way. (Okay, don't repeat that!)

2. What are you really good at and why?

3. What are your downfalls?

ACTION STEPS

1. If your defining word isn't clear to you, call or e-mail as many people as you know and trust—a close friend, your spouse—and ask these folks to describe you in as few words as possible.

2. Once you've narrowed down your list of words to five, bounce them off the people you trust. You are trying to find the essential word that best describes you. After working on the process myself, my word is energetic. What is yours?

3. Write your defining word in the first layer of your RYI chart (a blank chart is located at the back of the book or draw your own as we move along. Visit realyouincorporated.com for an interactive version).

A Real Story

Mary Ernst McColgan

Meet Mary Ernst McColgan, born in 1967, owner of
a floral design company, Rose Bredl Flowers. Business
owner since 2004.

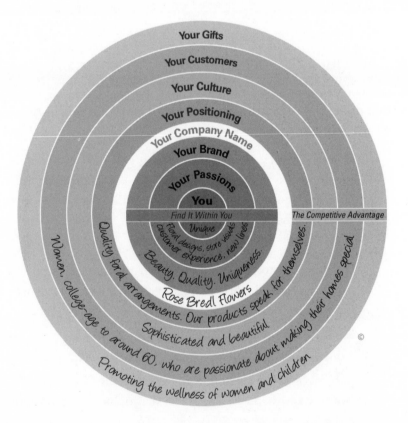

My real word is unique. *I come from a family of gardeners, especially on my mother's side of the family. I even named my company after my grandmother. I combined that family passion and my experiences working for a number of national retail chains—Estee Lauder and Abercrombie & Fitch among them—to create my business. I knew that with my background and drive, I would be successful as an entrepreneur. That, plus my eye for perfection and quality and a strong customer service background, gave me a lot of confidence.*

If my company walked down the street, it would be sophisticated and beautiful. It would stand out from others because of its quality and uniqueness. It's about style, and treating each customer as if they're your one and only. It's about the services we offer and the products that we use. All hand-selected from artisans across the country and other parts of the world. We refuse products that are mass-produced. Again, it's about quality and beauty.

We encourage customers to be hands-on. It's okay for them to get their hands dirty. That's our store and our brand, and those customers will make my company stand out. I believe our store and products speak for themselves, and our customers recognize the quality and work that goes into everything we do. My business is unique, like me.

While Mary knew her real word right away, it may take you longer to settle on yours. That's okay. It's the heart of your RYI chart, and it's important to get yours right.

RECOMMENDED READING

♦ *amBITCHous: (def.) a woman who: 1. makes more money 2. has more power 3. gets the recognition she deserves 4. has the determination to go after her dreams and can do it with integrity* by Debra Condren, Ph.D. Read it, and you may be inspired to choose it as your real word.

So far, we've established that it's all about you, and we've outlined the first life lessons to help you get started:

♦ Your future starts now

♦ Learn from your past

♦ Describe yourself in one word

Now it's time to move to the next layer of your RYI chart: Your Passions.

It's not who you are that holds you back,
it's who you think you're not.

Unknown

your passions

REAL FACT #2
Define Your Passions

You recognize passion when you see it, don't you? It's that sparkle in a person's eye, the spring in their step. Passionate people exude pure, real energy. Confidence and a sense of empowerment. Everything they say is infused with enthusiasm. We all recognize it—and hopefully—we all want it in our own way. The road to finding and remaining true to your passions is littered with life. Disappointments and setbacks abound, no matter your age or current work situation. We've all experienced them. The disappointments hurt our heart and dampen our fire. Did you know Lucille Ball was kicked out of acting school and told she had no talent? Of course, she went on to create her own show, cast her husband as a supporting actor, and formed her own production company. This talented and hilarious actress also turned out to be a savvy business owner. She never gave up, no matter what the "experts" said.

In this Real Fact, you will learn how to spot people I call passion poppers, folks masquerading as friends and confidantes who are really snarks in disguise. You will discover, like Lucy, that perhaps the best way to have it all may be by completely integrating work and family, since balance as a constant may be an elusive and unachievable notion. It's more of an ebb and flow, really. Read on for reminders of the power that flows from surrounding yourself with people whose passions connect with yours, and from following your instincts as you complete the second layer of the RYI chart. Specifically, you will learn to:

♦ Find the real people in your life

♦ Avoid going it alone

♦ Follow your instincts

Passion: That's what you're looking for.

Find what it is that makes you wake up and smile in the morning.

What elements of work put you in the best mood? Who inspires you? What encourages you?

If you already know what you want to do, and you are making a career doing it, you still need an occasional touch base with yourself. Are you on track? Do your decisions coincide with the real you in the first circle of your RYI chart? Are you following your passions? This Real Fact will help you make sure that's the case. We all know intuitively that our hobbies and interests represent an extension of our real self. But do these passions need to be relegated to the off-work hours of our lives? Nope. Following your true passions, creatively and uniquely, will bring true meaning to your work life. It's exciting.

? Did you know?

Happiness is linked to success, according to a University of California Riverside study.

Evidence showed a strong correlation between happiness and productivity, generosity and a stronger immune system.

You're about to discover the next layer of the RYI chart: your passions, and how to find what they really are. The first step lies in forging personal relationships with real people. Surround yourself with those who support you, think like you. To help get you started, you'll meet some real women who have followed their passions with amazing success.

Life Lesson Four: Find the real people in your life

Okay, so you know at heart the real you. You also know it's a jungle out there, so it's imperative that you surround yourself with support. By nature, women are nurturers—the ones always helping others. As you venture down the path toward entrepreneurship, you must establish a network of the real people in your life. You'll recognize them because they are real. They tell you the truth to help you, not to hurt you. They are family members, best friends, and co-workers. These true, real people in your life are so important because let's face it: The world still conspires against you if you're a woman starting a business.

You need a team. People you can call to raise your spirits, to answer your questions, and to help you move forward. These are your Real You protectors. They shelter you from the constant naysayers. They may even protect you from yourself when you're in the doldrums, consumed with doubt. It's unfortunate, but true, that we still have a long way to go, even though we've come a long way. And it's also true that for many women, and probably you, the way to shatter the glass ceiling is through entrepreneurship.

That said, you have to watch out for snarks, and find the real people in your life. To help along the way, I've devised what I call the Snark Scale. Hopefully, this scale will improve your ability to recognize the snarks all around us, and instead, fill your life with real people—friends, mentors, and such—who make you feel good because they think like you, share your passions, and empower you. Later on, you'll revisit this scale as you build your business and begin hiring. But at this early stage of finding your passions, the bottom line is this: If someone isn't supporting you and your passions, they are using you, draining your energy, and pulling you down. Remember, you're on a personal mission.

> To get where you need to go, separate yourself from negative influencers.

On your way to fulfilling your passion, the more real you become, the more polarizing you'll find yourself to be. If you're making waves and pursuing your passions, people notice. Real people and snarks. Your job is to distinguish between the two, and keep the snarks from bringing you down. Watch out for these passion poppers (see Snark Scale on following page):

Beware. As you are no doubt aware, the business world is filled with snark-infested waters. Snarks exist everywhere, but you can fine-tune your radar and pick out their special blend of snarkiness just as they pop into your life. And then you can get rid of them. Almost every day someone says something to me they would never say to a man. I was recently with a male attorney who was prepping me before testimony at a deposition. He told

The Snark Scale

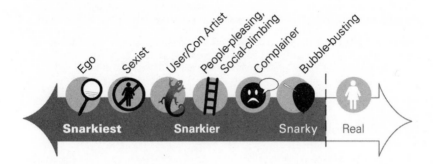

 Ego Snark

It's all about them. No one else's dreams, feelings, goals, or opinions matter. They don't think other people count. They will sit in a meeting with you and act like they support you, feign to be your friend, and then grab your ideas and run for the glory. They don't play fair, and they never will. Self-centered and self-righteous, these are the worst of the snarks and the most dangerous to your culture, and your passions. Why? Because they want what you have. All of it. They work methodically, and may even seem to be the best employee you've ever hired. You don't want them in your life or company. They are takers, not givers. Relationships are a means to an end; not an emotionally gratifying, mutually beneficial connection. They cannot change. They divide your company quicker than you can say, "Should we do a team-building retreat?" Unfortunately, with this type, you may be the last person to realize you have an Ego Snark in your midst. Typically, he or she has stepped on everyone else before finally coming after you and your job.

Sexist Snark

The purveyors of the grand male tradition, these snarks are largely responsible for unequal family responsibilities at home and inflexible and inequitable workplaces. Whether part of the old guard of sexists—overt, unapologetic, crass—or the new—cautious, undercover, seemingly supportive—these snarks are bad news for entrepreneurial women everywhere. While we've come a long way since the 1960s when most Americans opposed the expectation of equal pay for women, these snarks don't appreciate the growing equality in the workforce. (Women now make 77 cents for every dollar a man makes, according to the National Organization for Women.) Or they continue to push the question of how can you work when you have children, without, ironically, asking themselves the same question. When you uncover a Sexist Snark, run the other way. They won't change, and neither should you.

User/Con Artist Snark

Like higher-level snarks, these people are completely unreal, too. Think chameleon. Often these con artists are insecure and lack the self-confidence to be themselves—so they never are. They use their relationship with you for their own benefit, taking more than they give. They deceive others because they offer just enough support to not be a complete snark. They can act like your friend and often get along with everybody. They may seem like a team player, but they do not accept responsibility. These snarks can play games so well that you think they're being genuine. They demonstrate outward manifestations of relationship-building, but it stops there. Be careful. These snarks also are experts at using your contacts and network to their own benefit.

People-pleasing, Social-climbing Snark

Though not as dangerous as the other snarks, people-pleasers rarely serve as a great addition to your space or your organization. Unwilling to make unpopular decisions—or any decisions at all— these snarks also resemble a chameleon. They can change their outward demeanor and even their guiding principles to "adapt" to the audience and situation at the moment. They are always keeping score while acting like friends, because they are people pleasers and people collectors. They want to win the most-likely-to-get-a-raise contest—not for their performance, but because they are so nice. They don't want to give more than they think they should. And, bottom line, when anyone is spending this much time trying to be popular or avoid making decisions that could possibly upset somebody else, they aren't getting a lot done.

Complainer Snark

Remember Eyore in *Winnie the Pooh?* Whining doesn't seem that dire of a trait compared to the others, but influential complainer snarks are those people you like, but for some reason, you see vestiges of snarkism. Trust your internal barometer. Keep them close, but not too close. You will end up hiring at least one of these folks along the way, but they aren't lethal. They can be nice, pleasant, and get along with others. But you don't want a huge collection of them. They may jump on the team bandwagon, giving back more than taking, but they are likely mumbling under their breath if they disagree with a decision or worse, spreading rumors. These snarks will make it a point to find out insider information they can later put to personal use. Confidential information should not be shared with these folks.

Bubble-busting Snark

Find these people in your life inside and outside of the workplace. They're the folks—friends, family and others—who tell entrepreneurial working moms that they should really be at home raising their kids. Bubble busters tap into our deepest guilt—the working mom guilt, the "I'm being selfish" guilt—and the myriad of other internal guilts that diminish passion and cloud our dreams. Bubble busters are sneaky. They can even seem to be friends, but their side comments and under-the-breath criticisms leave you feeling cut to the heart. Don't confuse these passion poppers with real friends. You need to be careful how closely you let these snarks into your life. If you're stuck with them, be careful how much of your dreams you share.

me, "You need to act more professional, like a real president." He was referring, he said, to the fact I smile, don't dress in traditional suits, and, "well, other things." I told him, "I am a real president, and this is how I look. Period." It's not easy, but don't be afraid to stand up for what you know is right. Sometimes, the outcome may not be pleasant or what you expect—remember setbacks make you stronger, as you learned in Real Fact 1—but it can be a stepping stone for personal growth.

Remain true to your passions, despite snark attacks. That's the best approach to creating a real brand. Authenticity is the name of the game today.

Love who you are, and what you do. Do it all as a proudly passionate real female entrepreneur.

QUESTIONS TO THINK ABOUT

1. Who are the real people in your life?

2. Are there snarks in your life?

3. Can you remember a snark attack? What did you learn?

ACTION STEPS

1. Remember, you want to lead and make your own rules in your life and in your business. You've thought about the real people who can help you get there. Are they on your calendar? Make sure you routinely meet with them.

2. Write down the characteristics people most admire about you. Ask your real friends for help.

3. Take a look in the mirror. Are you trying to act or look like somebody you're not? It's the twenty-first century, and there are 69 million other women out there in the workforce. You have permission to be, act, think, and look like you. What does that mean?

A Real Story

Anne Murray-Randolph

Meet Anne Murray-Randolph, born in 1950, publisher

of *LORE* (Lives of Real Estate) magazine, the *People*

magazine of real estate. Business owner since 2004.

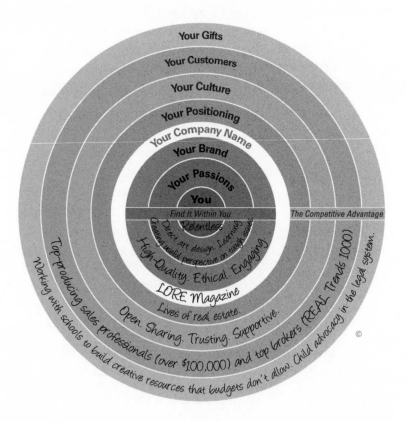

I've had several mentors who have encouraged me to throw myself into opportunities whether I had the right background or not, and to never fear failure. When you don't fear failure, if something doesn't work, it's only a little bump in the road.

As a fine arts grad selling copiers for Xerox, I was attempting to inspire Roy Simpson, an executive vice president with American Can, with the idea that color was a better communicator. I needed 45 minutes for my "pitch"; he gave me 20. I took a humorous approach talking at warp speed, flipping through the "deck" like a person on speed, and then he said: "Sorry, no time for questions." I instinctively knew he wasn't a purchaser. He said he wasn't enchanted with the copier, but he was with me, and asked me to come to work for him. He liked my spunk, the fact that I wasn't intimidated, that I had a sense of humor, and that I had already done things that included a lot of personal risk. He hired me away from Xerox and put me in many different roles to really "try my wings," including working on a high-barrier plastic replacement for the metal can. He also paid all costs for my MBA.

Another was Jack Eustace, my boss at General Foods when I started there. He pushed me beyond whatever analytical limits I thought I had and made me think past logical answers to creative possibilities that were really just wild hypotheses (something you just don't do at huge corporate entities). One of these crazy concepts allowed a division to bring more than $4 million to the bottom line, and I received the Chairman's Award for Outstanding Performance.

Finally, Dave Gustin. He hired me to be a director of new products at Frito-Lay. He was the first to realize that I mentally dual-processed all the time—working on problems in my subconscious while talking to him about other projects. I could then bring the issue to the forefront without thinking about it. He also was the person who recognized my ability in new product development. I saw things that other people didn't. I worked *with him at General Foods, then Frito-Lay, and then when he was head of Hunt Wesson, a division of Con Agra, when I had my own new product consulting firm. When I called him in the summer of 1994 and said I wanted to start my own new product development firm, his only question was how fast I could get to California to start working with his group. That first contract was worth more than $100,000.*

Anne's learned over the years how to keep the real people in her life, and how to avoid snarks. Collecting wisdom and lifelong friends along the way, Anne has excelled in her many businesses because she found the support she needed—from a motorized bicycle company (RevoPower) to an award-winning magazine (LORE). Other women have, too. According to the study titled "Paths to Entrepreneurship: New Directions for Women in Business," 46 percent of women business owners reported having a mentor or a role model whom they looked up to or drew encouragement from when they were starting their business.

RECOMMENDED READING

♦ *Flux: Women on Sex, Work, Love, Kids, and Life in a Half-Changed World* by Peggy Orenstein. Well, the title pretty much says it all. Read it when the passion poppers have you down.

Life Lesson Five: Don't go it alone

In life, and in business, you've got to play to your strengths. And if you're in the formative, dream stages of planning your business, you must be careful. Avoiding snarks and following your instincts both matter. So does the old adage, "Don't go it alone." As you begin to surround yourself with those who understand you and your passions, who believe in you, you may discover a partner for your business.

When I first began working on this book, I turned to many trusted, real friends who know my brand, understand my passions, and support my dreams. Among them, my editor, my husband, several members of my team at Real Living, and my friend, Sarah. Sarah just happens to be a fabulous writer with her own business, a former journalist and a wife and mother. I thought she needed something else to do, so I asked her to help me with this book. To me, having support on entrepreneurial endeavors is part of my passion. Kelly Kinzer Malone, at Real Living, jumped in and kept me sane, and she is another reason you're holding this book in your hands. I say at home, "It takes a village to raise a Rouda," borrowing from Hillary Clinton's book. It's true with this book, and really, every successful project with which I have been involved. Collaboration is—at some level—important for all of us. It's the notion of sharing—ideas, experiences, mistakes, accomplishments—and building something together. It's much the same for me at Real Living. My husband and I are partners in the business, and at home. To say it's equal and well-balanced everywhere would be a stretch, but we do complement each other and try to do the best job possible of leading a business, growing wonderful little people and trying to stay real.

Trust is essential, and, increasingly, people find that trust is the secret to successfully working with family.

If it doesn't kill you, it will make you stronger.

There is an ever-growing number of husband-and-wife teams running family-owned businesses. According to *HR Magazine* (1998), experts estimate that between 80 and 90 percent of all businesses are family owned. And in a 2003 report released jointly by Babson College and the MassMutual Financial Group, their study found that women-owned family businesses are almost two times as productive as those owned by men. It's almost full circle from our agricultural roots if you think about it. Back when most Americans were family farmers, family meant working together, playing together, growing together, and surviving. Family businesses composed the majority of all businesses.

The 1950s confused everything with ideology and falsely defined male-female positioning in society. Before the world wars, men ruled the private, public, and civic sectors. During the wars, when the workforce needed women, it was all about working as a team. When the enemy was gone, women were forced to take a back seat. These artificial distinctions between men's and women's roles have taken a long time to break down. They still exist, but we're making progress. Sure, not everyone chooses to work after marriage and motherhood. But if you do decide to build your own business, doing it with a family member—especially a spouse—is frequently a more common choice. Finding a compatible business partner is never easy. Finding someone you can share both a bed and a company with—well—you can do it! The key is role definition. Who assumes responsibility for what functions?

Then there's the potentially toxic problem of who has the final say on the big decisions. And of course, there is the always-present question of how to keep work from consuming your life, especially if your life is your shared business. I've found that every partnership thrives through clear role definitions. But with a family member, it is imperative. If it's your significant other as your partner, the stakes are higher all around. A couple-owned business represents an emotional and financial risk. But when it works, there is a unique reward in being part of a power couple.

Real estate abounds with husband-wife, mother-son, mother-daughter teams, and more. At Real Living, my husband is the CEO, and I'm the president. We didn't reach this partnership easily or lightly. We had a few bumps in the road, and even a master manipulator in the middle. But, for the most part, I decided if I'm going to build a business again, it might as well be with the person I'm building the rest of my life with. Here's just a bit of what we've learned so far about working with family, whether it's a spouse, sibling or other (see figure on following page):

Oh, and it's not easy. But it's doubly rewarding, when things are going well—and doubly frustrating when they aren't. Keeping our eye on our collective vision helps. So does the fact that we've clearly delineated responsibilities at work and at home. It doesn't, of course, change the fact that there is too much to do and too little time, every day. With four kids, one dog, two cats, a bird, and various small amphibians running here and there, along with the constant judgment from the outside world—including, in my case, a number of folks at the office who are uncomfortable with a husband-wife scenario—and the general internal guilt for being a working mom, things can be tough going at times. And then there's the fact that by your mid-40s, there are the added societal pressures to remain youthful, look great, have a fulfilling career, make it to every kid's sporting event, try to be Martha Stewart at least once a week, and eat dinner together. The constant pressure—much of it self-imposed, much of it pushed onto us as women—to be it all, do it all, have it all, take care of it all—leaves little room for introspection, especially once children are in the picture. But it is crucial you do so. Life also zooms

Insist the family member gain work experience elsewhere before joining your team. This gives your family member more credibility—even though he or she will be constantly judged based on their relationship with you. Remember, you are the boss, and it's your real brand at stake.

Be sure to delineate clear roles and responsibilities. Ensure that your family member is qualified for the job and try not to provide special favors, or conversely, hold them to a higher standard.

Keep the personal out of the business—and vice versa—as much as possible.

by, and keeping your real brand at the forefront is always in everyone's best interest. The real people in your life know that, and will validate it. Don't get isolated when life gets crazy. Reach out. Stay connected to an assortment of friends and colleagues. And remember to nurture the Real You in the center of the chart even as you take care of everyone else.

Considering a partnership with a nonfamily member? According to bizstats.com, 72 percent of all small businesses in the United States are sole proprietorships. But that doesn't mean there aren't successful partnerships springing up everywhere. Much like with family members, the rules of engagement must be clear, and I would urge you to avoid a 50–50 split. Someone needs to have the final say, and since this is *Real You Incorporated,* that somebody needs to be you. That said, though, a business partnership with a person who has skills complementing your own is a perfect scenario as long as you both share the same vision for your company. You'll create the essence of the company, but your partner needs to understand, agree, and embody it. Make sure the business rules are defined up front. Get a business attorney involved early on. In today's knowledge economy, it's a wonderful benefit to not have to go it alone. A partner can provide synergy and complementary ideas and skills. But these relationships should not be taken lightly, or without documentation. Just as business partnerships can ruin family relations, they can ruin friendships, too.

But remember, whether your partner is a family member, a friend, or a business acquaintance, this is your Real You Incorporated dream, first and foremost. I'd encourage you to finish this book, at least the first section, before you begin discussing your partnership. You're on a path to self-discovery to illuminate your business dreams. Finish Section One, and use it as a map against which your business partnership brand will unfold. Because if your prospective partner doesn't get the Real You and what you're trying to bring to the world, the relationship is doomed from the start.

As you begin to think about, or rethink, your Real You Incorporated business, you need to stay assertive and strong. It's your passions, your dreams. Whether you choose a partnership or sole proprietorship for your business, you can't accomplish your dreams by yourself. But that doesn't mean you need to compromise. Just remember, you're not picking someone to save you, but support you. This is your dream. Always remember, whose company is this? Who's number one?

QUESTIONS TO THINK ABOUT

1. If you are considering a partnership for your business, would you consider a family member? A friend? Or do you want a sole proprietorship?

2. In your dream of a perfect world, how integrated do you want work and home life to be? Be sure to think about your present and future holistically.

3. If your life were spent pursuing your passions, would it have more significance? How can you ensure your entrepreneurial passions complement and nurture the *you* in layer one of the RYI chart? In other words, what makes the *you* in the first circle feel great? Your passions ignite the first level.

ACTION STEPS

1. Write your perfect job description. Play to your strengths. Read some online job postings for ideas.

2. What are your weaknesses? Can a partner or family member enhance your skills? Who's the strategist and visionary? Who's the deal maker? Is that you?

3. If you are considering a partnership, create a breakdown of the roles and responsibilities. A real brand is created with realistic and clear roles and responsibilities. Start now.

A Real Story

Meredith Liepelt

Meet Meredith Liepelt, born in 1969, owner of a marketing firm for entrepreneurs, Rich Life Marketing. Business owner since 1995.

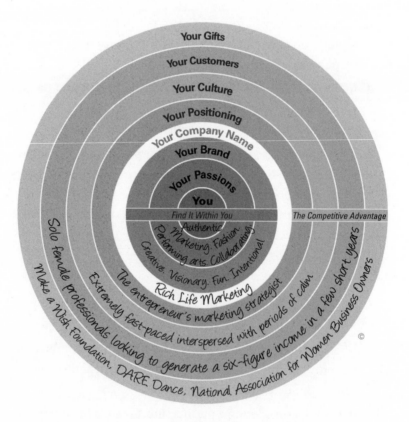

I started my career as a corporate recruiter and eventually moved into human resources management. I worked in HR for almost 10 years, and then I wanted to do something else. I decided to marry my career in management with my lifelong interest and participation in the performing arts. Consulting worked very well for me because I was able to continue my work from home after I started my family.

After the birth of my first baby, I accidentally started another business. I was making some interesting burp cloths for myself, and the idea caught on quickly with my friends and family. Before I knew it, I was selling to baby boutiques and specialty gift stores across the country. I enjoyed a growing list of celebrity clientele, and my products were selected for the 2006 Oscar® Nominee Gift Bags!

After a lot of soul searching, I sold my business and realized that what I enjoyed most about it was the marketing. In fact, I generated more ideas than I could implement. People from all over the country who had read about me called and wanted my advice, and I found that I really thrived on helping others with their marketing. I am truly passionate about helping other women in business, and although my new business is very much in its infancy, it's already thriving.

Throughout my business ventures, I've had several mentors and continue to cultivate new ones. When I first started my baby accessory company, I had no experience with producing a product, so I reached out to other entrepreneurs who helped me realize that if I really wanted to do this, it would be a lot of work—but it would also be very rewarding. My first mentor was a woman who is younger than I am and makes unique soaps and bath items. My next mentor was a business consultant in New York City who I hired to help me formulate my business plan. I maintain a relationship with her, and she provides me with insight into many aspects of business. Over the past year, I have been working with a life and executive coach. She helped me realize what was right in front of me the whole time—that I am passionate about marketing! I would not be where I am today without my mentors, and in return, I have also mentored others along the way and will continue to do so. I firmly believe that you can't receive guidance without also giving it. The formula is really quite simple: You grow as you give.

One of my top tips for a woman starting her own business is to get out of your office and start talking with people. You can't run a successful company by sitting in front of your computer.

A great entrepreneur, Meredith learned early on that you can't launch and operate a successful business in a vacuum. She benefited from the experience of others when she was launching her business, and is still reaching out to others as her business grows. Her point—and an important one: Ask for help when you need it and follow your dreams.

Recommended Reading

♦ *Inside Every Woman: Using the 10 Strengths You Didn't Know You Had to Get the Career and Life You Want Now* by Vickie L. Milazzo. In other words, go for it, just don't go it alone.

Life Lesson Six: Follow your instincts

As a current or future woman entrepreneur, you're uniquely capable of blending your personal passions with your professional goals. Women are master multitaskers. We're also especially talented when it comes to putting other people's needs and wants first. Too often we do what others tell us to do, sometimes blindly obliging society's expectations for us. Is that what you're doing? If so, how is your heart feeling? I'm guessing not so good. When we compromise our dreams, our passions suffer. But when you follow your instincts and take action, as difficult as it can be, you uncover a career bursting with fulfillment instead of frustration. Eighty-five percent of women entrepreneurs are optimistic about their business's outlook, according to a National Foundation for Women Business Owners study.

While following your instincts sounds simple, others' opinions and the process of living our lives can blur our true passions. This is another chance to take a step backward. Think about what you dreamed of becoming when you were a child. When life was all about possibility, what was your vision? Those first dreams tap into the heart of your passion, your talent. Those pursuits that are so innate to you are uniquely yours.

In the first Real Fact, I shared my experience about learning who I didn't want to become as a business owner, based on some bad boss and work experiences. Similarly, I had a number of great bosses whom I would later emulate. What's the lesson here? Follow your instincts. If the place you're working makes you uncomfortable, it's not a good fit. Period. Find a way out. Take charge. Make it your choice. No matter your circumstances, you do not have to stay in a bad situation. Make a plan and get out. There are always options. Some might say my personal real brand took a big blow by being fired from my first ad agency. Wrong! It only made me stronger. The fact of the matter was I had left a fun job in radio to pursue my dream of working for an advertising agency. I just happened to pick the wrong one. You learn more from adversity than the everyday routine, right?

Okay, so I was out of work, it's the start of a new year, and I am living in my first apartment and now suddenly, I'm paycheck-less. In a nutshell, times were tight. I started networking immediately, careful to show people a person in control, a person who was out of a job, but confident that she would land on her feet. I told people the truth about what happened at the agency, and why I left. It's okay to say you've been fired. Your brand can handle it. As I looked for my next job, I continued as a freelance writer for a city magazine and other publications. I contacted my former boss at the restaurant and asked if I could start waiting tables if my savings ran out before I found another job. (I had about three months of a cushion.)

This time, I was much more selective. I followed my instincts and my written objectives that by now I was able to articulate to myself. I knew I would visit only agencies I would consider working for, not just be wooed to join one based on a fancy, and at that time, an alcohol-fueled power lunch. I was going to find an advertising agency with a culture that suited me, that felt right—and I knew by this point, that it meant a place where I could wear pants. At the very least, I truly hoped I would find a place where my brand would fit. Creative and caring. Energetic, but focused.

Did you know?

You should always follow your gut. Scientists from the University of Amsterdam found that the best strategy for decision-making is to gather all of the information, put it aside for awhile, and then go with your instincts.

I found that with my first true mentor, Nancy. She had created a PR firm with a culture I'd imagined, and she offered me a job the day before I was to start back at the restaurant. Whew.

Nancy knew happy employees need structure and freedom, challenge and kudos. She taught me how to have more confidence in my choices, and I loved watching her in client pitches. She had grown her division of a large regional advertising agency into its most successful business unit. Resumes flowed in the door daily. She was able to be selective, and everybody who worked there felt lucky to be part of the team.

So the attributes I liked about Nancy are some of the things I try to emulate in myself and business. She was strong, creative, and willing to take risks. Those are the things I took with me. And working for Nancy was a path to my passions. I wanted to write, be in the advertising industry, and be creative. As a kid, watching *Bewitched*, I was entranced by Samantha and her creative power, and I wanted Darrin's job. Now, I was on my way, or so I thought. Problem was, I didn't enjoy most of our accounts. I liked working with entrepreneurial businesses—places that embraced creativity, not process. We had a few of those, but mostly, we had big corporate operations like McDonald's. Sure, I learned a lot. But, there was always a way things had to be done. A process. A lot of rules. During this period, I learned another important lesson for my Real brand. I don't like artificial structure, or processes without purpose.

To keep my creativity fueled, I launched Hobson Communications. I still worked my full-time job, but I took some local and regional writing assignments and even became a stylist for a national magazine's home section. I didn't know anything about styling a home for a photo shoot, but I learned along the way. I trusted my instincts, and that helped me through. At this point, my small business was just an add-on, a way to add some creativity to my writing and marketing life. It was a start, and I followed my instincts to do it. A designer friend of mine created my first business card. It read: Writer. I smiled. No rules on that card, just possibilities.

QUESTIONS TO THINK ABOUT

1. Earlier, you thought about the real people in your life, those closest to you. Now it's time to branch out beyond the personal level. Who are your heroes? Who inspires you?

2. If you could be anyone else for a day, who would it be? What is your dream?

3. What are the things you are most passionate about? What business activities feel most like fun and least like work? What makes you smile?

ACTION STEPS

1. Write down the names of three of the people you admire most. They can be family members, strangers, celebrities, whoever. List three characteristics you admire about each.

2. How closely do those attributes and talents match the heart of your passions? Do you recognize the real you in them? You should see similarities in the traits you admire about each and record them.

3. Write three to four of your passions in the second layer of the RYI chart. These are uniquely your passions. No one can take them away. It's up to you to make them come to life in your real brand.

A Real Story

Anjel McLaughlin

Meet Anjel McLaughlin, born in 1970, owner of AKADA Hair Salon. Business owner since 1997.

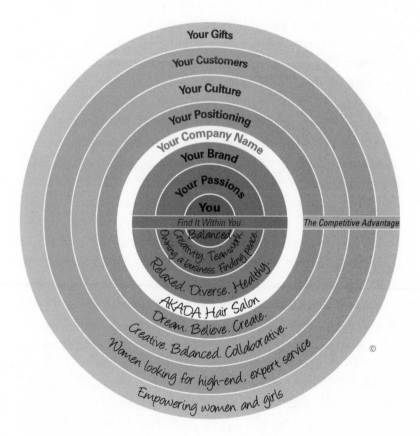

I wanted to do what I love to do in peace. I also wanted to create a healthy work environment. To me, that means harmonious. Before opening my salon, I worked for three different men and each of their companies was so ego-driven that they didn't care about the people working for them. I got so tired of it. I wanted a place where I could come in and do my job, do it well, leave at the end of the day and not be worried about the stress and bullshit. I didn't want to feel like I needed a stiff drink after work every day.

When I started my own business, I was too pissed off to be scared, and I had nothing to lose. I wasn't married. No kids. I left because the man I worked for cut my salary 20 percent over the course of the year because he thought I was making too much money. When I quit, he said I'd never be anything without him. So I brought my mug with the logo on it from that salon, and I drank out of it every morning just to remind me of those words. "Okay, thanks," I said every morning. It tasted good.

For me, the best thing about owning my own business is earning the respect of my employees, my people. Something about being able to not become so focused on the bottom line that you sacrifice the human aspect, the humanness of business. I think respecting the people who make up your company, and hiring people whose opinions you value, not just people who agree with you, but people who say what they mean, is key. I like insight from different personalities. It gives a more balanced spectrum when you allow people to have a voice. Hire diverse people, and everything is expanded. You expand who you are, you expand your business. Asking for input in how to run the place has been really great. And definitely hire people who are different than you. I look for people who are balanced and respect the value of differences, and see those as good qualities.

I think I'm a better boss because I'm a woman. I understand the necessity of balance for a healthy life. Family doesn't need to be compromised just for the bottom line. It's not to be confused with soft. I'm fair, and I'm honest. But it's not frou frou either. I think you can get the job done and not be a zealot. I don't allow the egos you see in other salons. I like collaboration. On purpose, I didn't name the salon after me. I wanted it to be bigger. To be a company, because I think it makes the employees feel more a part of it. I do value collaboration among creative people. For problem solving, the solutions you come up with collectively greatly outweigh all the ideas of just one person. So far, it's worked out great.

Anjel is all about doing what feels right, going for it. She is passion in action. Her success is a reminder that whether by accident, necessity, or by chance, many female entrepreneurs are born. For Anjel, now it seems a natural choice, and she can't envision fulfilling her passions otherwise.

RECOMMENDED READING

♦ *The Naked Truth: A Working Woman's Manifesto on Business and What Really Matters* by Margaret A. Heffernan. Heffernan is one of the pioneers of women business empowerment. Her book is very insightful about why women have left corporate America and become entrepreneurs.

There is much to be learned by the paths chosen by each of the women profiled in this Real Fact—and about the people we admire. They teach us about solidifying and embracing your passions, about finding the right path, surrounding yourself with real people to launch your dreams and stay true, and following your instincts. As women, we have more freedom than ever before, and the collective power to make our lives work the way we want them to. Knowing yourself and what you want goes a long way toward feeling in control. But never be too proud, or too afraid, to ask for help.

Create a business and a life that is a reflection of you, your goals, your dreams, your essence. Then, when the challenges come—and they will—you can return to that essence and know it was worth it. And it will be, because you chose it. Congratulations, you're two steps into the process. In this Real Fact, you've learned to:

♦ Find the real people in your life

♦ Avoid going it alone

♦ Follow your instincts

In the next Real Fact, we'll discover your brand, wrapping up the first section of *Real You Incorporated* as you continue to Find It Within You.

The way to gain a good reputation is to endeavor to be what you desire to appear.

Socrates

your brand

REAL FACT #3
Discover Your Brand

Whether you're working for someone or a business owner, you've had work experiences just like mine. In fact, these kinds of experiences explain, in part, why such a large percentage of business startups belong to women. No matter how far you have traveled in your career path, you have the power to create your own individual, personal brand. Create it and nurture it while working for someone else. Set it free when you start your business. And it won't be the same for everyone. As we keep reminding you, it all starts within you. And grows as you follow your passions until finally, your business emerges as a real brand. Look at the first two layers of your RYI chart. These layers start to articulate your tempo, your ego, and your personality.

Now, let's work on formulating or solidifying the vision of the real company you're creating. In this important Real Fact, you will discover your brand. This means being able to tell your company's story, even if your company doesn't exist yet. It calls for you to define your brand essence, the critical last words for the Find It Within You section of this book. And it involves crafting your vision statement. This is where your dreams begin to solidify. It starts with these life lessons:

♦ Tell your company story

♦ Define your brand essence

♦ Create your vision statement

Life Lesson Seven: Tell your company story

You've uncovered the one word that best describes you. You've identified your passions. What other steps should you take to get to the essence of your brand? It's much the same as the process you've been following with defining yourself. Just as you have a past and a core essence, so does your business. Trace or imagine the history of your company. Tell your company story. Think about what problem your company was designed to solve, or, if you're still in the planning stages, what problem should it solve? Is it a lifetime dream? There is a truth there somewhere, just itching to see the light of day, and it's not, most likely, about profit. (Of course, you know this well if your real brand is a nonprofit organization. But have you become so mired in the tough business of fundraising that you have lost track of your true essence?) Remember, this is about your company's genesis, your business's personality.

Whatever the company's origins, document them. Write them down, videotape them, or, if you aren't creative, hire someone to do it for you. If you are taking over a business, get the founder, your predecessor, on tape now, before it's too late. I'm not talking about ad footage. You don't need to discover or promote the next Dave Thomas, and your brand doesn't have to be Wendy's size. (Although when Thomas spoke for Wendy's, that felt real, didn't it?) And, if you're a startup, begin to save things. Save the notes you have jotted down as you work through this book. It's really that important. You get the point. This exercise is your company's scrapbook. Capturing its history. It's crucial to your essence. It's your business roots.

Most business stories don't need to be elaborate, but they do need to be recorded. At the end of the day, it's all about you. That means your personal brand and your business's brand are one and the same. At the heart of it, a real brand helps build the business and life you want by creating a conscious culture of your choosing. If you're in business, you have a culture, an identity—as does your business. Your business comes to life as a brand. It has a history and an essence. Dig it out by extracting and documenting the key milestones, memories, and ideas.

I created the name Real Living originally as the name of our real estate company's first e-newsletter in the late 1990s. Back then, HER Realtors in Columbus, Ohio, was my husband's family business, and I served as an occasional marketing consultant. With the decision to try to grow the business nationally in 2001, we sought a brand name that would work for the future, speak to our target audience— women, who continue to be the majority of the real estate industry's sales force and control or direct 91 percent of all residential real estate transactions—and act as an umbrella for three Ohio-based companies we were merging together. We decided on Real Living—a name that spoke to the future of the company we were

Did you know?

In early 1989, Dave Thomas began appearing TV spots for Wendy's. After 13 years (and 800+ commercials) later, Guinness World Records™ recognized the Dave Thomas Campaign as the "Longest Running Television Advertising Campaign Starring a Company Founder."

shaping, while also honoring the past. The word *real* tied us to *real estate,* but it also stood for something more. Living is what you do, and we wanted to be the company people chose for much more than the actual buying or selling transaction.

If your Real You Incorporated company is a startup, have you thought of a name?

Naming your company matters.

As you ponder the life lessons in this Real Fact, no doubt you will find inspiration. If you already have a name, just focus on discovering the essence. If you need both, let's get going. To remind yourself of your real brand, you will be filling in the name of your business in the layer separating the two sections of the RYI chart.

The first step is to record the story. This is important. To bring employees into your company and have them understand and represent your brand, they need to know the real story. At Real Living, our employees and agents are part of something much bigger, dating back more than 50 years. To know that, and share it with buyers and sellers, is important and key to making brand fans.

In 2001, when the companies were merging, I took the opportunity to write a combined company history. Each was a well-documented business success. The Cleveland company was launched in 1953. The Columbus firm came to life through my father-in-law in 1956. Both companies were initiated by male entrepreneurs. Both became market leaders. And both—fortunately—engaged dedicated administrative, marketing, and training folks who saved photos, mementos, and otherwise scrapbooked their history and successful growth of each brand. For the merger announcement, we printed and distributed a combined history book, for our agents across Ohio who suddenly became part of a new, bigger entity called Real Living. We wanted to celebrate the past, and demonstrate how each made Real Living what it is today. We're in the process of creating what it will be in the future. But I know where to turn to find the milestones and celebrations along the way. It's part of our company story.

When I think about successful women entrepreneurs with a clear real essence personally and a defined real brand professionally, I'd be remiss not to mention Oprah Winfrey and all she has accomplished. From defining her career her own, real way—as an extension of her personality—while being so successful in the many brand extensions she launches, from business ventures to philanthropy, she is amazing. Her success is due, in large part, to the fact we feel we know her. Oprah directly shares her story, personally and professionally, and the story provided the foundation for an empire. She has created and defined her real brand. So now it's your turn: Tell your story.

QUESTIONS TO THINK ABOUT

1. Did you know many successful retailers write a story for a concept brand before it even launches? It's true. These creation stories bring a nonexistent company to life with a made-up history and culture. Yours, of course, should be based on your reality—the first two layers of your chart—but can be embellished, of course.

2. Have you gathered the imagery to document your roots and beginnings? Gather everything from early photographs to brainstorming doodles.

3. Are you keeping in mind that even if you aren't the founder, you are now in charge, and your real brand all starts with you?

ACTION STEPS

1. Your company may be an extension of you, but its story remains distinct from yours. What is your company's story? Write it, in 250 words or fewer.

2. Make video recordings and digital photos of your humble beginnings now. It will make you smile later. I promise. Open a new document and call it "My company story."

3. Take the time to list all of the people who have played a significant part in your business so far. You don't want to forget who to thank later.

A Real Story

Sue Doody

Meet Sue Doody, born in 1934, owner of an American-style bistro, Lindey's. Business owner since 1981.

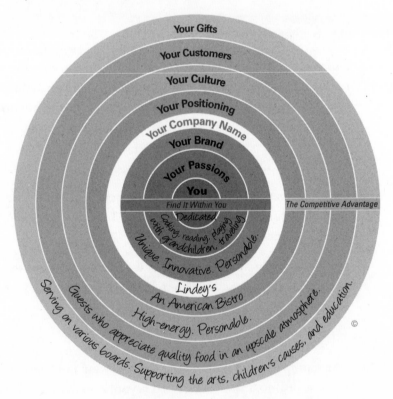

I always knew that I wanted to do something after my four children started school, but I was not quite sure of what I wanted it to be. After I was divorced, the decision to do something was made. I always had a great love of cooking and started to give gourmet cooking lessons in my home. I also did some catering for small events and businesses. My children always appreciated my cooking and felt that someday I should have a restaurant. I was about 40 years old at the time. Julia Child was my mentor and inspiration, along with her TV show, The French Chef, *and her cookbook,* Mastering the Art of French Cooking. *As I look back, the decision to begin my own business was made out of necessity and to realize a lifelong dream.*

My company's brand essence can be summed up in three words: unique, innovative, and personable. It is my belief that people should be welcomed like they would be in someone's home, and we should attempt to meet their every need. My personal brand is to maintain consistency of product and service and attempt to get better each day. My business is a reflection of my business goals. The Lindey's team knows my expectations and philosophy and strives to carry that out.

My family and I just completed a book about my company, As the Table Turns: Biography of a Bistro. *Looking back, I probably waited too long to document Lindey's, but like many entrepreneurs, I was so busy growing my business, I just didn't take the time. But I lucked out. Lindey's is such a visible place in our city's history that stories and news clippings were everywhere. Once word got out my family and I were working on this project, we were inundated with information. I think the book is important to document what's been accomplished. Lindey's is a well-known restaurant with many longtime customers. It's another connection for them. It's also a great marketing tool. People outside of central Ohio can now have the opportunity to learn more about Lindey's. Our history—my business's and the employees and customers—is a rich fabric of personal stories and shared experiences. It makes us what we are today and proud of where we have come from. It is invaluable to have it documented. I hold the book in my hands and smile.*

Sue's experience is unique. Most companies, yours included, probably don't or won't have a large group of raving fans who create an instant history and provide scrapbook elements of their company's history. You can hope that happens—or you can take the necessary steps now to get your history, as it stands now, on paper so you don't have to imagine a future without it. With her personal and business history written, and a cadre of trusted friends and employees at her side, it is a relatively easy process for Sue to articulate her company's brand essence. I hope it is the same for you. This is a crucial step. Once defined, it is important your three words are solid. True. Real. Bounce them off as many people as you can, whom you trust. Read on for more.

RECOMMENDED READING

♦ *As The Table Turns: Biography of a Bistro* by Sue Doody, is a great memoir, company history, and cookbook.

Life Lesson Eight: Define your brand essence

Ready to fill in the third layer of your RYI chart? It's time to describe the culmination of your life experiences and dreams, and use them as the logical jumping-off point for your company. You've written the company's history. The next step is to define your brand essence, the words you'll use to define your business to the rest of the world. Ultimately, it's your company's personality. Brand essence is a collection of intangibles—attributes that make your company unique and different. You've read about brand essence in several entrepreneurs' real stories already. Sue's brand essence sums up as unique, innovative, personable. Anjel's brand essence comes alive as relaxed, diverse, and healthy. In case you're not sure where to begin, sit down with a blank sheet of paper, a whiteboard, alone or with a few trusted colleagues, and begin to write. Start with words that pinpoint what you want to create and reflect your core beliefs. If it's an existing company, be sure to embody the positive characteristics that exist. If creating from scratch, enjoy your blank canvas.

Can you define your business in three words? Is it real? Does everyone know it, feel it, believe it? What are the immutable facts about your company's history, or if you're just starting, what is its vision? When we combined three companies in Ohio to create Real Living in 2002, one of the companies was headed by the founding father and son-in-law, another was led by the founding father and his son, and the third was guided by a management team. All came together, participated in a brand essence workshop led by an advertising agency, and forged an agreement about the core beliefs of the stakeholders of the three companies.

Here is a chart (see below) of all of the words that burst forth in our brainstorming session. It demonstrates how the three words we selected for our essence encapsulated many other words and values we'd discussed.

We deliberated, talked, laughed, even cried—a full, three-day exercise—and I'm happy to report, most in the room were true to their beliefs. At the end, we agreed that, based on past success and future plans, *family, innovation, and results* should be the hallmarks of our future. Great, we thought. Now we're ready to move forward. We had a strong foundation in place. Unfortunately, half of the stakeholders from one of the companies, including the founder's wife and daughter, never came to the table. While positioned as silent partners, they were, in fact, quite active

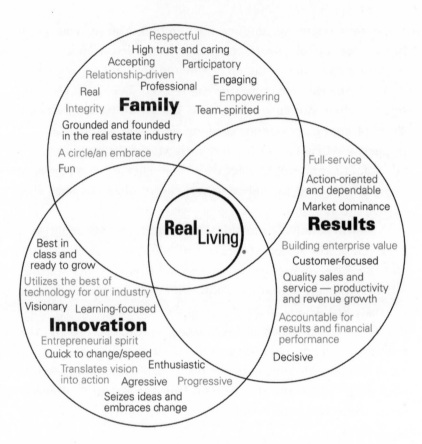

in the company. Their lack of inclusion in the branding process eventually led to the spin-off of that division.

We learned the hard way to include all strategic stakeholders in a merger situation. When you set out to form an open, honest, true brand, invisible leaders and secret agendas can bog you down. So try your best to find out who they are up front. Let them go their separate ways at the beginning rather than further down the road.

As an entrepreneur, you ultimately define the essence of your business. You may ask others to help you along the way, but please avoid snarks, and limit the input to a dozen or less.

Brand essence by committee is tough. Remember, the goal here is to get to the heart of things. Sometimes this process can seem overwhelming. If you feel you're heading in that direction, consider working with outside third parties, like an advertising agency. Unbiased, educated opinions can be worth their weight in gold.

Finally, the exercise must be democratic. In a privately held business or even in a publicly held corporation, it's vital to get input and buy-in from all of the stakeholders, even if they are typically invisible in the day-to-day operations of the business. These words form the core of your hiring decisions, the parameters by which you generate and judge every thing you do. They lie at the heart of what your business is, and what it will be.

QUESTIONS TO THINK ABOUT

1. At Real Living, the stakeholders worked with an advertising agency to come up with the company's brand essence. That was necessary because of the size of the merged companies. Would outside counsel be beneficial to you?

2. Who are the core stakeholders in your real brand? Make sure you include every one of them, now, because it's too late later.

3. Have you searched the Internet and made sure the brand you're thinking about doesn't already have a URL out there? It's an easy check. They can't take your essence, but someone may have registered the name you want.

ACTION STEPS

1. What are the three best words to sum up your brand's essence? Write them on layer three of your RYI chart.

2. Capture the words you didn't choose to use down the line for marketing purposes and vision work.

3. If you haven't selected a name, what do these essence words say to you?

A Real Story

Tripti Kasal

Meet Tripti Kasal, born in 1962, owner of a real estate franchise, Real Living Infinity. Business owner since 2005.

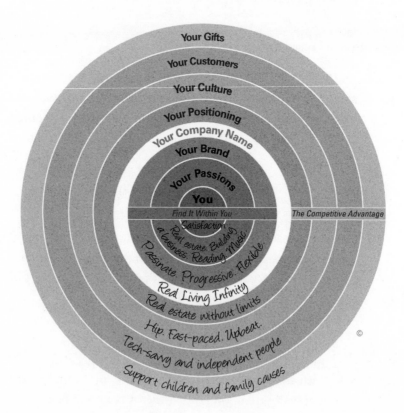

Right out of college, I was a computer programmer for a couple of years when I started to realize that I would never be happy working at a desk job or working for someone else. Ever since then, I have been involved in entrepreneurial-type pursuits of one sort or other, primarily in and around real estate. I spent about three years as a sales manager for a real estate company, with the goal of learning how to run a real estate office in order to allow me to own my own company. Those three years once again confirmed that I am happiest when I am making my own choices and not working for someone else. Although my business card now lists my title as President, Managing Broker, I have always thought it would be cool to have business cards printed with the simple title of Entrepreneur *under my name.*

My name, Tripti, is the Sanskrit word meaning satisfaction. That's probably a good word to describe me. Not in the sense that I am satisfied, but in the sense of seeking satisfaction. My passion is real estate—I love everything about it: the financial and investment side and the people side of it. I also enjoy building a business, reading, and music. My business is passionate, progressive, and flexible.

My company's name is Real Living Infinity, and my tagline is "Real Estate Without Limits." The name is about endless possibilities in real estate, but also in future endeavors and life in general. It's about abundance.

One of the best things about being a business owner and an entrepreneur is that my home life and work life are fully integrated. This did not happen by accident, but by choice. When my kids were young, I had a home office built in a spare room. The concept of actually creating a separate space to work at home was relatively unheard of back then, but it enabled me to work from home and still be aware of what was going on in my children's lives. I absolutely believe in work-life-family balance. It's like a three-legged stool. If any of the legs are missing or even a different size from the others, the stool cannot stand. The entrepreneurial lifestyle has been key for me to achieve this balance.

Tripti's story is exciting. First, she nailed her personal and company brand essence and found a unique and enticing name for her company. Next, she added a tagline encompassing her vision. She's also managing a fully integrated work and family life. You can, too. These center layers of your RYI chart define your future. Life Lesson Nine will help you with the final step of this section.

RECOMMENDED READING

♦ *Bird by Bird: Some Instructions on Writing and Life* by Anne Lamott. I reread this book whenever I need writing inspiration. It is perfect.

♦ Another great source is *Writing Down the Bones: Freeing the Writer Within* by Natalie Goldberg.

Life Lesson Nine: Create your vision statement

Through the Real You Incorporated process, we're going to share with you not the *how* to write a business plan, but the *why.* There are many resources you can turn to—software, online, books—to write a vision statement and a business plan. This is something more, deeper. This is the notion that you are inventing your real brand based on your personality, your passions, your beliefs. And from those ideals flow the business of your dreams. You first, business next. Whether or not you're currently running a business doesn't really matter. It is never too late.

It wasn't for us. In the beginning, Real Living was a collection of individuals committed to family, innovation, and results. But our company, like yours, needed further definition and that's where the vision statement comes in. You need to bring your real brand essence to life. I'm not talking mission statements, those syrupy, verbose, and many times, plastic, statements companies overused in the 1980s and 1990s to connect with people. The era when those statements emerged from boardrooms across America and then were passed out to employees, consumers, and shareholders like doughnuts at an all-company meeting is long gone. Thank goodness! Today, philosophy and purpose statements last with consumers about as long as an ice cream cone on a hot summer day.

A vision statement, on the other hand, brings the future and goals of your real brand into focus for everyone. It is how you paint the future, the dream for your company, and bring it to life through a story. From the get-go, Real Living was created to change the face of residential real estate. But what does that mean if you weren't one of the leaders in the room that day? If you didn't take part in the brand essence workshop? Not a lot. That's why we needed to build a vision statement.

At Real Living, we had our three essence words: *family, innovation, results.* We wanted to create the next national real estate brand. We knew it could be different, more real, and presented in a manner that would reach out to women homebuyers and sellers. Our company was created from the merger of *real* real estate companies, and we always kept the needs of the real estate agents at the heart of everything. We also know real estate is filled with entrepreneurs, and those are the type of people with whom we wanted to grow and connect. After much wordsmithing, we conceived what we think is a great vision statement: To become the nation's leading entrepreneurial, agent-centric, consumer-focused network of real estate professionals built on family, innovation, and results.

Strategy Map

Vision

To be the nation's leading entrepreneurial, agent-centric, consumer-focused network of real estate professionals built on family, innovation and results

Human Perspective
(Building Intimacy and Accountability)

Real Living promise to agents
To be the best in:
- Business Planning
- Technology
- Marketing

Real Living promise to employees
- inspire you to do your job at your fullest potential
- align your role with the company's initiatives
- create an environment where you are challenged and can grow
- offer innovative, employee-centric programs and offerings
- provide a place to work where Monday is like Friday

Branch manager promise to agents and Real Living
- Brand in field
- Recruit
- Develop + retain
- Make a profit
- Run the office

Agent promise to consumer
- Share information
- Personalize the experience
- Organize the process
- Save records + documents
- Care about the relationship after the sale

Brand Promise

Real Living promise to consumers
Real Living:
- is relevant and real
- will help you find your dream (home or career!)
- will help you relax, and genuinely cares about your well-being
- is aspirational, friendly, engaging, smart and savvy
- knows what you want and need before you do
- will help you find ways to make your home better for you and your lifestyle
- will stay a step ahead of your technological and lifestyle demands
- will help you find your balance (work-life, buying-selling, and more!)

We also created a strategy map anchored by our vision, with responsibilities flowing from each group within the company to one another, and to our customers as we began building our business together.

A vision statement acts like the road map for your real brand. It's a game plan for you and your employees to rally around and bring to life. It all starts with you, your belief in where you're going, and how you see the future. And then your vision comes to life through the statement. Your vision statement can be different from your marketing positioning statement and probably should be. Your marketing is external; your vision is an internal message.

QUESTIONS TO THINK ABOUT

1. Think about the long-term goals for your business. Are you creating a national brand or a fabulous community business?

2. Who are your core internal audiences going to be? Employees? Independent contractors?

3. What do you want to provide to them?

ACTION STEPS

1. Write down your three essence words. Keep them handy.

2. What other adjectives do you want to associate with your vision? Leading, best, full-service, unique, trusted, different, others?

3. Write your vision statement. This is one sentence. Play around with it until you feel inspired.

A Real Story

Sandy Clary

Meet Sandy Clary, born in 1946. Owner of a communications firm, Clary Communications. Business owner since 1983.

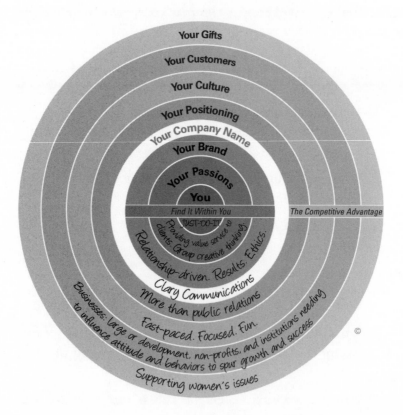

I think I always knew I wanted to be an entrepreneur. I don't think it is something you do, it is something you are. It's an adventure I wouldn't trade for anything in the world. Here, almost 25 years later, I am still learning new things every day. That's what makes it such a treasure.

We've done quite a bit of visionary work at the firm. It helps us define who we are and who we aspire to be. Encapsulating all of this in writing helps us build our brand, just as we're building brands for our clients. It helps us stay focused and on task. The creation of our vision was a team process. For everyone to have a stake in it and understand it, they had to be involved. It is our vision that Clary Communications be a leader in the evolution of public relations as a primary strategy in building brands and driving business success.

Our firm's culture is fast-paced, focused, fun, and very creative. The essence of my business is relationship-driven, results, and ethics. In the office, I have a passion for providing value service to clients, group creative thinking, and securing new business relationships. Members of my team must have the perfect combination of attitude and skills. Passion for our industry is a must. With that comes a dedication to mastering the skills needed.

As a sole practitioner, it made sense to put my name in the company name. What more of a commitment can you make to a company than to put your name on it? However, as the years passed, I regretted that decision, because my company is so much more than just me. The name does not adequately recognize the many talented people who have been part of making my business a success.

As Sandy makes clear from her story, the ability to rally your troops around a vision makes all the difference. It's imperative that they buy into the concept. She sets the tone with her vision, gives marching orders and never looks back. She also offers a great message about the name game: Consider what it means to the rest of your company if your business is named after you. Could be good or could feel limiting. No matter what, vision is key. Get yours right, and make it actionable for your business.

RECOMMENDED READING

♦ *The DNA of Leadership: Leverage Your Instincts To: Communicate, Differentiate, Innovate* by Judith E. Glaser. It's so hard to describe, and she does a great job. Intuition in action. Unstoppable.

The culmination of your life experiences, your dreams, offer the logical jumping-off point for your company. Now that we've covered this Real Fact's life lessons, we've completed the Find It Within You section of *Real You Incorporated*. Altogether, you've learned to:

♦ Realize your future starts now

♦ Learn from your past

♦ Describe yourself in a word

♦ Find the real people in your life

♦ Don't go it alone

♦ Follow your instincts

♦ Tell your company story

♦ Define your brand essence

♦ Create your vision statement

You've completed the first three layers of your RYI chart. Congratulations! So what's left? Plenty. It is time to jump into Section Two: The Competitive Advantage. How do you leverage your personality, your passions, and the essence of your brand into a uniquely you enterprise? That's what you'll discover next. Read on.

SECTION II

The Competitive Advantage

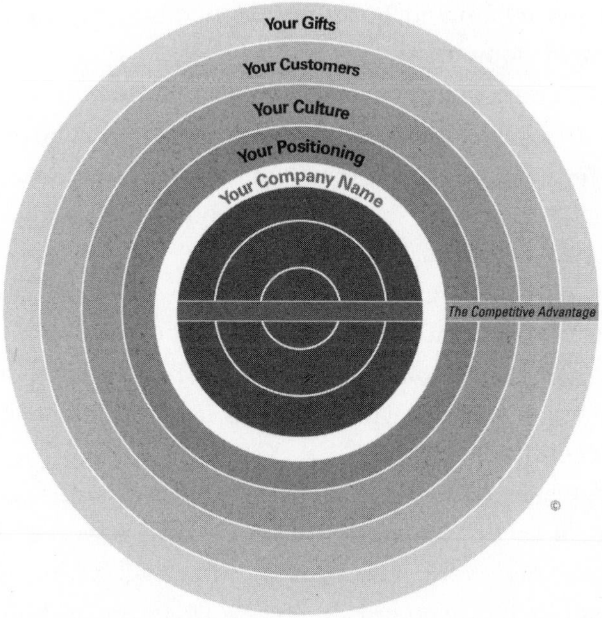

In the first section of *Real You Incorporated,* you found your Real brand within you. By starting with your dreams, your goals, your personality, and your passions, you've completed the first three layers of your RYI chart and documented your personal brand.

Now that you understand your personal brand, it's time to turn your attention to your competitive advantage within the business community. You bring a unique business perspective to the world. In this section, we'll define a process to help you share it.

In Real Fact 4, we'll cover marketing and the importance of branding. Quite simply, you cannot have a successful business without having a brand. It's either defined by you up front, or it gets created along the way.

Your culture is the focus of Real Fact 5. How do you define yours, hire to it, and keep it positive? Your cultural goals should be to value creativity, to express your brand in hiring, and to avoid culture vultures. At the end, we'll ask you to define your culture in this level of the chart.

Your personal brand and your business brand are one when it comes to your customers, so in Real Fact 6, we'll help you pinpoint how to define your target audience. Real Fact 7 reviews the importance of building your business network and articulating your philanthropic passions.

And finally, *Real You Incorporated* leaves you with a gift, a final Real Fact of inspiration. You've found it within you, and you've defined your competitive advantage. Your chart is complete—a big accomplishment. Your future is bright, and your creative energies are focused. In a nutshell, you and your Real brand are unstoppable. Real Fact 8 reminds you to enjoy yourself along the way.

So, jump in! Let's get busy articulating your unique competitive advantage as you deliver your Real You Incorporated brand to the world.

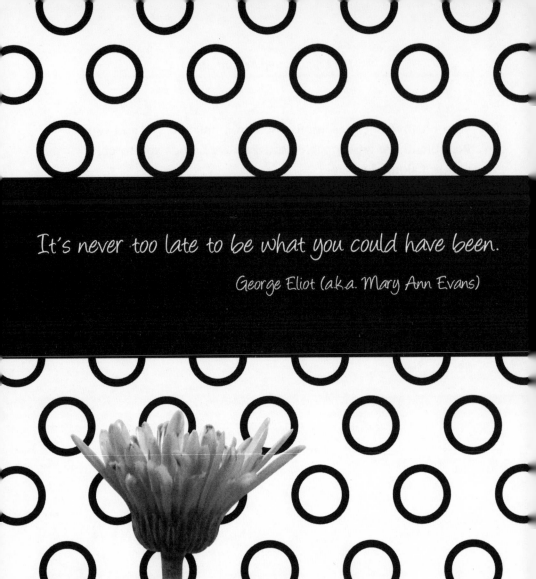

It's never too late to be what you could have been.

George Eliot (a.k.a. Mary Ann Evans)

your positioning

REAL FACT #4

Bring Your Passion and Your Brand Together

Real brands, like great restaurants, have floor presence. Imagine a fabulous Italian bistro downtown. You know the one with the owner's name in lights above the door. The owner-operator cherishes your presence from the moment you walk in the door through the meal to when the check is presented. Or think about your favorite clothing boutique your. The owner keeps track of your previous purchases and knows your likes and dislikes. Shopping in her store is something you look forward to—a fun experience, a treat, not a chore. In these restaurant and shopping scenarios, you feel cared about, respected, and embraced. It's different. You are having *real* experiences. Your patronage is appreciated. Valued. You smile when you arrive and when you leave, with perhaps a pat on the back or a hug. The essence of the experience is much more than good food or new clothes—although that's expected. Something makes you keep going back again and again.

That something is a real brand delivering on its promise. In the restaurant analogy, the owner gets it right by serving tasty food in a warm, personal environment. In the clothing boutique, the retailer has created a retreat, a sanctuary where customers feel comfortable and inspired. Of course, the problem for both of these businesses comes when the owner wants to, say, go on an extended vacation, or even retire. Is the business sustainable without that individual's personality? Real brands are, if their culture becomes bigger than the founder and the brand comes to life through all who are part of it.

How are you going to position your brand in the world? That's the fun of creating a real brand. It matters. For now, and for your future. In the first three Real Facts, you figured out where you are going, and how to keep your personality and essence part of your company's future. Now, it's time for some marketing. In the last Real Fact, you learned how to discover your brand essence—that intangible list of qualities and traits that makes your business uniquely yours. And we pointed out that vision and mission statements when created in a vacuum or pushed down from above don't work. It's living and breathing your unique real brand every day that makes a difference, and that is where the heart of marketing lies.

In this Real Fact, you'll learn about:

♦ The five senses of branding

♦ Creating a marketing plan

♦ Making it tangible

Life Lesson Ten: The five senses of branding

This is where the art of marketing comes to light. A Real brand incorporates all of the senses—sight, sound, smell, touch, taste—to create a unique position in the world. Creative perfection happens when your brand is passionately executed and fully integrated. And to do that, your brand needs to acknowledge all the senses.

Just as you started with a blank canvas and began encapsulating your personality to leverage it in your business, with the five senses of your brand, you have infinite possibilities with a new brand—and plenty of room for improvement if you are updating an existing company. Whether you're launching or repositioning, the same principles apply. This really is the fun part. Even if you don't consider yourself a creative type.

Most people are visual communicators. When you think of a brand, begin with the visual basics—symbols, colors, fonts—and build from there. Go to the bookstore and buy a lot of magazines. Not just business magazines, but lifestyle magazines, home decorating-shelter publications, as they call them. Grab a copy of any industry trade publications you can find to see how others in your space are positioning themselves. And then, have fun online. Print out home pages that speak to you, research the meaning of colors and shapes, and discover the meanings of certain colors and consumer responses to them. This process is similar to what an interior decorator will tell you to do when you begin working with her. She wants to get a sense of your likes and dislikes before she helps create your brand at home. You need to do the same to create your brand in the world.

Pick your color or colors. Primary and secondary colors should be one of your first steps in marketing and building your brand. Color choice will help guide the tempo and tone of your brand and will help as you work with a designer to create or refresh your logo. You'll be surprised how your real brand emerges from that fundamental color choice.

Next, find type treatments you like, fonts that speak to you, and print them. Cut out photos of people who look like your target audience, your potential customers. Clip different textures of paper or fabric that have the right feel. Yank out shapes you are drawn to, tear out ads you like. This is the fun part. Don't edit yourself; let your imagination run free. Build a brand board, or two, or three. You could make one for each of the five senses. Use regular poster board paper and start creating. These are idea starters for the brand you want to create.

See the following page for an example of a brand board I created for Real Living.

When I was creating a brand for a utility connection Internet startup, I was going through this process. I liked the notions of speed and convenience associated with the service. But in an intangible business like being a middleman for electric, gas, and cable companies, I also wanted to incorporate a feeling of friendliness and personification. My oldest son, who was eight at the time, had a pet tree frog. Jumps, as he was called, loved to ride on my son's shoulder. He would often hop from that spot to my laptop screen and watch me work, his sticky frog feet glued to my screen. That's the true definition of stickiness.

Well, inspiration is everywhere, as they say, and jumphome.com was born. The new company's materials featured a friendly illustrated tree frog—drawn by an illustrator from photos of Jumps—and two shades of green were the brand colors. The brand materials carried the positioning phrase: "Moving from pad to pad? It's free and easy as a hop, skip, and a jump." Suddenly, we had a fully positioned, unique brand with loads of personality, in the form of a frog.

At Real Living, we're round, red, and real. We picked a circle for our logo to symbolize the fact we're all-encompassing and friendly. Circles represent attributes considered feminine. In a sea

of squares, our brand stands out. We're red, because it was the common color of the founding brokerages, and I've already explained the *real* part, the essence of our brand. So how do you make round and red tangible? How do you stimulate the five senses and make an emotional connection to your brand?

As a real estate company, Real Living has a lot of yard signs—the purest representation of the brand in the field, visual communication at its most basic. But how do you make a service tangible? While out to dinner at a restaurant in South Beach, I noticed the use of blue stones sprinkled around, on the tables, at the host stand and the like. As you left the restaurant, they encouraged you to take one with you for good luck. Buying a home is the biggest investment most people make in a lifetime, so I decided we needed some tangible brand tokens of our own, and Real Living Rocks were born. The rocks come in three different colors—red, clear, and white—and symbolize, in order, energy, clarity, and enlightenment. Our agents present them to customers as good luck tokens. You'll find them at our offices in vases, sprinkled on conference tables, or in individual bags of three with our brand message at the closure.

Another touch point of the Real Living brand is the lava lamp. If you look up the definition of the first official lava lamp, you'll learn about primordial ooze and being in touch with all types of positive, deep energy. Of course, lava lamps also are a generational bridge—you'll find 60-year-old agents and 12-year-old children of clients with Real Living lava lamps on their desks at work, or at their homes. In fact, red lava, up close, became our first television commercial. Our 30-second spot featured the words "find, feel, know" and "Buying or selling your home? It's got to be real" floating within a sea of red lava. The spots broke through and are used today by our new franchisees when they are announcing a new real estate company is in town. In our corporate headquarters, you'll find several 12-foot-tall lava lamps and many others of all shapes and sizes adorning desks and conference rooms.

If your real brand doesn't have a smell, give it one.

It can be as simple as potpourri or as complex as picking a scent. There are companies blending smells for corporations just like perfume for individuals. It's a retailing secret that needs to be extended to your brand. Taste is another interesting branding challenge, especially for a service business. But what I refer to here is not so much making sure you have a company cookie, but perhaps you do have a thank you gift with thought. We surprise new franchisees with giant fortune cookies—expressing our thanks and good wishes for their future success. For another company, I made branded lollipops. Use your imagination. This is the fun stuff.

Okay. Sight, touch, smell, and taste. Sound is another key. What does your real brand sound like? At Real Living, we sounded like Cheryl Lynn's "It's Got to be Real" for the first year of our brand. It was great. Until Clairol's hair coloring unit started using the song, and then the *Shark Tales* animated movie came out with the song and, well, you get the point.

So, it was time to move to another song that captured our brand essence and, fortunately, a member of Real Living's creative team wrote one. You hear it when you call and get put on hold. You hear it on our TV and radio spots. It plays as our online videos load, and we're having it made into a ringtone for our cell phones. Before and during events, our song takes center stage. The lyrics weave in our brand essence words and our vision statement. The song itself encapsulates our brand, and it's a vital part of touching the five senses. When I was a marketing executive for a national home services company, the first thing I did was create a jingle. To me, music says a lot. It conveys emotion in a way words alone sometimes cannot. So get busy, and name your tune!

Once you've covered the five senses, there's one final important component of the creative process you need to create: your positioning statement, which is a package of words that communicate succinctly to the external world who you are.

When it comes to your positioning statement, think of it as a rock that anchors your marketing strategies. Your positioning statement is the external version of your internal vision statement. Take a look at all of the words you've used to create your brand essence in the previous section, and bring them to life for your customers. Nationwide Insurance is "On Your Side," and now the company reminds us that "Life comes at you fast." Think along the lines of "King of Beers" for Budweiser, "The New Generation" for Pepsi or "The Real Thing" for Coke. McDonald's is happy, Volvos are safe, and so on. You have defined your personality, and now you're defining your brand's—a key part of brand building.

What do you want to tell your customers through words? Be inspirational. Powerful. Persuasive. Express your unique selling proposition. Imagine your brand walking down the street. What does it look like? And most important to your positioning statement, what is your brand saying? What is its attitude?

At Real Living, our brand essence is family, innovation, and results. Our vision statement is: "A network of the leading real estate companies built on family, innovation, and results." Our external positioning statement is: "Buying or selling your home? It's got to be real." Because we purposely chose a name that encompasses more than just buying and selling homes, it was important for our positioning statement to include those words. We are, after all, a network of residential real estate companies. It also was vital to include the phrase, "It's got to be real." Not only were we implying a choice—choose us—but also the notion of real. Our brand essence. A promise of a true, professional service from our agents to our customers, and a real difference customers can feel. Authentic. Truthful. Transparent.

The important thing to remember is to have fun as you explore the creative and artistic side of branding. Perhaps your positioning already is clear in your mind: "We sell widgets cheap." That is certainly one way to go. But if you can include an emotional hook, all the better. "We sell *wonderful* widgets" gives you a lot more room for creativity and definition, don't you think?

QUESTIONS TO THINK ABOUT

1. What are the creative elements of your brand? What is its color, feel, shape, smell, and sound? These elements become your brand attributes.

2. Take a look at advertising around you that speaks to you. Think about why you like certain images. What songs are you drawn to? Which web sites do you find appealing?

3. What are the action words you associate with your real brand? What is the primary message you want to convey to

your customers? Use inspirational, persuasive, and powerful words. This is your call to action, your sell line. Remember to look back to your brand essence, because some of those words may be right for your external audiences.

ACTION STEPS

1. It's time to determine the creative attributes of your real brand. You know its name and essence, but what is its color? Next, think about shape. Do any speak to you and your company? Symbolize it? On to the sounds, feel, taste, and smell of your real brand. Imagine these elements and how they can help you bring your brand to life. Select everyday objects related to your brand. Think of something you could hand someone and have her make a connection to your real brand. To help you along the way, research colors, go to the bookstore and buys lots of magazines, visit the fabric store or art supply store. Start clipping, collecting, *dreaming*.

2. Make a brand board. Capture the colors, objects, sounds, and the rest either in a box or assemble them on a board or boards. During the creation of Real Living, I carried the brand elements around in a box. Literally. Until I could bring it all to life, I knew I needed the physical elements to help me along. Give it a try.

3. Take the words you used to describe your brand essence in the third layer of the RYI chart, and use them to write your positioning statement in the fourth layer of the circle. What's your line? What words summarize the product or service you are bringing to the world? Make sure it's the truth, based on unique benefits. This is a chance to relay emotion through words. You can do it.

A Real Story

Lisa Stein

Meet Lisa Stein, born in 1962, founder and CEO of an
Internet-based medical equipment business, SpinLife.com.
Business owner since 1997.

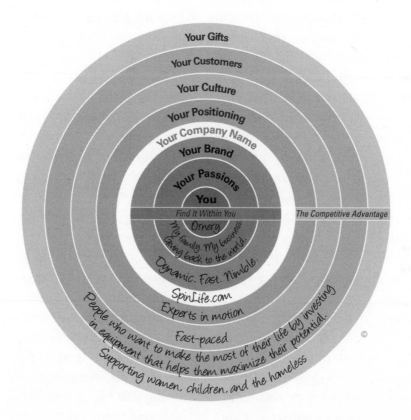

For me, becoming an entrepreneur was genetic. My grandfather founded a meat processing business. Then, my dad ran it. I spent 10 years working for other companies, but my plan was always to run my own business. It never occurred to me that you would work for others except to get experience that would help you go out and do your own thing.

One of the catalysts for finally becoming an entrepreneur when I did was an experience I had in corporate life. I had worked hard to build a strong and inventive new product and then a corporate decision completely unrelated to my division radically changed the direction of what my team was building. I didn't want to give power to someone else to control my destiny.

At SpinLife, we set out to change the way home medical equipment is sold. Three words that describe my business are dynamic, fast, and nimble. We have a quote by Mario Andretti on our office wall that sums up the way we think: "If things seem under control, then we're not moving fast enough." We feel as though we accomplish in three months what it would take most companies a year to do. That is the Internet pace. If I had to create a visual image of our brand in the world, it would be a titanium lime green wheelchair.

My background is marketing, specifically product design and market research, so I created a marketing plan at the get-go. I can't imagine starting a business without one. My advice is to realize the importance of the Internet in business today, and focus on understanding how the Internet and technology play a role in your industry. Our goal was to sell a lifestyle. Our competitors had a warehouse approach. We recognized the power of the Internet and used technology to create a web site with a positive image—hip, cool, dynamic, and loaded with great information and products. The result was a better experience for the consumer. Our point of difference was all about branding and design. If you don't know what your brand is up front, you don't know your business.

Lisa did a great job of finding a business niche—mobility equipment—creating a brand name—SpinLife—and crafting a positioning statement that clearly defines her offering: Experts in motion. Her brand has spunk and personality—you can envision it rolling down the street in lime green titanium wheelchair. When it comes to the five senses of branding, Lisa is on a roll.

Recommended Reading

♦ *The 22 Immutable Laws of Branding* by Al Ries and Laura Ries. A classic. Great tips. Easily digested.

Life Lesson Eleven: Create a marketing plan

Every business, large or small, has an identity. It's there, whether it's purposefully created or not. Whenever you have a collection of people creating a product or service, you have a company and a brand. And yes, advertising campaigns can put a shine to a dull brand, or add a temporary surge in demand to a formerly undifferentiated one. But creating true, lasting and successful brands in today's creativity- and technology-driven world is more about authentic beliefs than it is about the newest product or service. To create and sustain a real brand, people inside and outside your company must believe in you—not just your product or service—and find it relevant, dynamic, and tangible. A well-created marketing plan can provide you with a road map to build and sustain your brand's identity. It will help you focus, organize, and deliberate your actions and be efficient with your resources. It's the tool you use to propel your vision statement forward—and bring your positioning statement, which you just wrote, to life.

Creating a marketing plan for a business is my expertise. A marketing plan at its most basic consists of defining your positioning statement, outlining your advertising and communications strategy, specifying an environmental branding strategy, and yes, creating a budget. An objectives-driven marketing plan will tell you how much it's all going to cost, and quantify your success measurements. If you haven't done a marketing plan before, this life lesson isn't going to tell you everything you'll want to know. There are plenty of great books delving into the topic, and there are, of course, wonderful marketing firms and counselors. Even with more than 20 years in marketing, I relish outside counsel. It keeps me on my toes, and I learn a lot. So, whether you create the plan, or do it with help, the point of this life lesson is your real brand won't flourish without one. Just as having a good accountant is important to your entrepreneurial efforts, so is having marketing advice—and a sound marketing plan. There are just too many constantly changing variables today to keep up with. New media distribution channels emerge daily. This is great news for you—costs are going down and measuring the success of your advertising dollars is much easier. Consider this: in 1966, there were five media distribution channels: TV, radio, newspapers, magazines, and the eight-track. By 1986, there were 12. Today, there are more than 30 traditional, digital, and mobile media channels, and that number seems to grow daily. Many of the best marketing opportunities for your business exist online. The possibilities are exciting— and can be overwhelming.

So while you're looking for your marketing partner and thinking about your marketing plan, here are some basic first steps to get you started.

First, register your name and your company's name as a URL, and register your trade name and trademarks at the federal and state levels.

Second, Google yourself. Do you know what's out there about you already? This may seem obvious, but brand building in the fully integrated and connected world of today starts and ends online. Before you spend any more time building your Real brand, make sure nobody else is already using it or can take it away. I am in the unfortunate position of not taking my own advice. I'm currently battling a cyberstalker to get my name returned. While I spent the past six years building the Real Living brand, I overlooked this essential and easy method of personal brand building. It goes without saying that Internet adoption rates have ramped up to the extent that there is no identity without the Internet. Ergo, register your name. Grab a few different spellings. If you are Jane Smith, it may be too late. But if you are, like me, a woman with a distinctive name, you should be fine.

Real Living's 360° Marketing Integration™

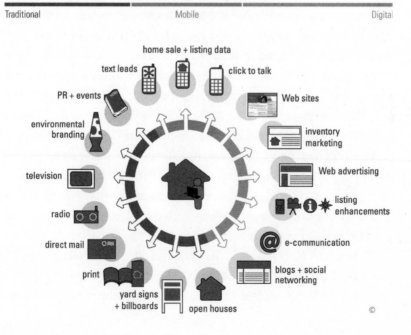

Next, keep it simple. Strategies and tactics can get confusing, so I've always hearkened back to what I learned as a young marketer. We are educating our owners and managers about what we're calling 360-degree marketing integration. It is the notion that today's businesses have a myriad of advertising choices between traditional, digital, and mobile. And it's imperative you select your advertising venues from among a mix of all of these tactics. For your industry, the choices are most likely similar. The point is the mix.

Lastly, don't get hoodwinked. For example, I've witnessed a search engine marketing firm tell a startup businessperson that all she needed to do was invest in a pay-per-click campaign, and she would receive a mountain of online leads. Business would boom. It's not that simple. Online sales reps have many counterparts pushing traditional media as well. I've seen other small business owners succumb to the promise of brand building through sponsorship, especially in sports venues, and they watch as their one tactic for advertising doesn't drive the returns promised. Advertising in general has always been about the mix, and that hasn't changed. Never put all of your eggs in one basket, and don't forget the basics. If marketing your business on opening day means you have only a logo, letterhead, a one-page web site, and a business card, so be it. Put your web address and e-mail address on everything, and build a robust web site as soon as possible. Don't get overwhelmed, and never think advertising anywhere replaces the power of one-to-one marketing. Nothing will ever replace the power of communicating—by e-mail or at lunch—with a potential customer. Personal marketing. You are your brand, and your brand is you.

While it's important to understand all the different media tools available between traditional, digital, and mobile, you also need to understand the purpose of each adverting message.

Advertising takes place on three tiers: image, sales promotion, and events.

Think about image advertising as positioning your company to its target audience. The messages conveyed in your image ads should include the essence of your real brand. Anchored with your logo and your positioning statement, image advertising puts your best foot forward. Think of it as deserving at least half of your marketing budget as you are getting your business established. You need to let everyone know your real brand has come to town. This is your brand out for a walk. Typical venues for brand image advertising include print, such as magazines and display ads in newspapers, and broadcast television, where even today the reach is unbeatable. Digital media choices for image advertising include banner ads, where you have the room and chance to strut your stuff. When you are thinking of your image tier of advertising, your biggest opportunity is your online office: your web site. That home page needs to say it all. Think about whom you can link your web site to. What online and offline associations make your brand look its best? That's where you should be placing your image advertising. Local media outlets' web sites are often a good choice for your image banner advertising, especially if you can work a deal including traditional television advertising.

Sales promotion, the second tier of advertising, is what you do when you have a price, an offer, or a "hurry, act now" type message. This type of advertising is less about your brand and more about the offer or product. A great media choice for sales promotion advertising is online search marketing. Think of advertising on Google or Yahoo! or MSN today much like you would have thought about the Yellow Pages a decade ago. Businesses appeared for free in the White Pages—as long as you had a phone number. Today, with a web site, your business will appear organically on the search engines. It may not appear on the first few pages, but it will be there. To assure attention, many businesses spent and still spend, considerable dollars on Yellow Pages advertising strategies, and that's very similar to today's paid search marketing through engines such as Google AdWords. Search engine marketing is an entire discipline, and learning enough to make decisions is critical.

Other distribution channels for your sales promotion offers include traditional media such as direct mail and e-marketing tactics such as e-cards and e-mail offers. Mobile marketing offers numerous direct marketing choices, and its popularity will continue to grow. No matter the media choice, the message and how it is conveyed must remain true to your brand, and carry your web address. In the world of spam, make sure you have permission to call or send e-mail—or you'll be in trouble. Targeted, permission-based marketing is the rule today.

Event-based marketing begins with your open-for-business celebration and goes from there. Many advertisers have turned to virtual events of late, tapping into social networks. While those strategies are effective, again, there is nothing better than one-to-one, person-to-person interaction. If you organize and execute a great event, it can go a long way toward marketing your business.

If you decide to include events as part of your advertising strategy, remember all the details. And be aware that events are a lot of work. One of my favorite client products from my advertising agency days was Frosty Paws dog ice cream. We spent a lot of time creating events to draw dog lovers and their pets. Picture taste-offs in grocery store parking lots across the country. When it came time for Frosty Paws to debut at the Fancy Food Show in Chicago, we had the booth set up, great dogs lined up, but we needed a mascot to compete with the Planters Peanut guy and the big M&Ms. We decided a Miss Frosty Paws would do the trick, and I was assigned the task of casting the model, which I did. There was just one problem when she showed up. She was maybe five feet tall in heels. In a sea of towering mascots, Miss Frosty Paws was underwater. So, I learned when casting to always check details, like height. Events to promote yourself, your business, and your product or service remain one of the best ways to reach out and touch your customers. Just stay true to your real brand. And make sure every detail is executed with perfection.

So how do you incorporate all three tiers of advertising when you're just launching a business? We faced that exact problem with the launch of Real Living in 2002. Our marketing budget was small. With it, we created a home page that was really nothing more than a simple online brochure. In fact, we had to use most of our marketing dollars to secure the URL, realliving.com, from a company in Tennessee. We had our brand essence and positioning statement defined, and we knew we wanted to change the face of real estate. We knew our target audience. We had a marketing plan. Since we were launching a new brand on top of two existing, 50-year-old companies in two different media markets, we launched focusing on the image tier. We used a broad range of 360-degree media choices, including the 30-second lava lamp television broadcast and cable TV spots, radio spots with our song playing prominently, newspaper and magazine ads that were very red, banner ads, e-marketing, including e-newsletters and e-cards, and more. To garner attention to a brand launch, broadcast television and cable are still great channels, and coupled with online, great at local market penetration. We called the campaign the "Changing the Face of Real Estate" campaign, and many of our new franchisees use the same creative today as they open a new market and paint their towns red.

And what about communications' role in brand building? It's vital. Use public relations (PR) to help position your brand in both the traditional media—print, radio, TV—and digital—blogs, social networks, online news services. Components in a PR strategy include press releases (your message), target media list (whom you'll send it to) and strategic pitches to make journalists want to write and talk about your company. In many cases today, content-strapped news outlets will use your press releases verbatim. Media relations, part of PR, has changed, but it's still important to get your real brand's story out. Do you know reporters in your market? If you're an online play, do you know the bloggers or online trade publications that cover your industry? Get to know these folks. We often advise our new franchisees to begin with media relations, a relatively inexpensive way to announce you're in town and you're open for business. And, of course, invite them to your events. They may not show up, but the gesture is a good one. Many successful dot-coms leaped to the top of the Web's most trafficked sites through media and public relations strategies alone. We recently retooled our corporate relocation division at Real Living. To put a fresh brand polish on an existing division, we relaunched the web site and drove the new look and brand solely through a media strategy targeting workforce reporters and human resources trade publications, in addition to our standard media list. Never forget the power of the pen—or keyboard.

? Did you know?

In November 1999, DoubleClick Inc. said its DART (Dynamic Advertising Reporting and Targeting) technology hit a new record serving one billion ads in a single day. Just consider how many they are serving now…

Source: Veronis Suhler Stevenson. 2007

Another important piece of your marketing strategy is your environmental branding plan. It's so important, and often overlooked. In fact, I've dedicated Life Lesson Twelve to it in this Real Fact. Environmental branding cements the image of who you are in your customers' minds. It's beyond your advertising and includes everything from your office environment to the signage on your building.

Your marketing initiatives need to include both online and offline components. Today, you must replicate all physical and offline strategies online. Try a blog, for example. Launch your business with a page on Facebook or whatever popular social networking site you choose. With mobile, digital, and traditional advertising, there really is no such thing as any purely offline business. For your brand to be successful, you've got to have an online presence.

Beyond your web site, you'll need to consider whether the other media tactics make sense for you, including blogging, video, and social networking. And while you're dreaming about and planning your brand's appearance, or freshening it up, don't forget the third screen. Mobile marketing is in its infancy but growing in reach, power, and options daily. If you are selling a product or service, chances are you'll need to think of a real brand strategy for mobile. It can be as simple as formatting your web site for mobile PDAs or as complex as a fully integrated mobile marketing campaign.

Don't panic or get confused by the ever-growing array of options; just be aware. When you need help—the speed of change in all industries today is exploding and marketing is no different— ask for it. And while your real brand's marketing objectives, strategies, and tactics will be different from mine, hopefully I've provided some examples to get you started. The basic point is: Keep it real. If you are uncomfortable with a phrase or an image, it's not true to you. And if you don't understand something, research it. At the touch of a button, you can Google a definition, find a template for a marketing plan. It's all available. You make it yours by staying true to your RYI chart. Bounce ideas off your essence, your passions. That's how you know if you're being authentic. Follow your intuition, keep your customer in mind, and go for it.

QUESTIONS TO THINK ABOUT

1. Do you feel comfortable writing a multitiered marketing plan, encompassing messaging for all levels of advertising, communications, events, and more? Or are you taking a more basic approach and just jumping in? Either way, it's critical to identify your advertising budget early on.

2. Do you have a vision for your web site? This is often your most important office. What does it look like? How is your real brand conveyed online? Is it purely business? Purely informational? Transactional? Engaging?

3. Think about companies and brands you like and are drawn to. What are the common elements in their advertising and

communications strategies? Where do they advertise? Can you discover their media mix? What captures your attention? Find some role models, in your industry and others, to watch and learn from.

ACTION STEPS

1. Register your name and your company's name as a URL. Today. Google yourself, and set up a Google alert for yourself and your company, and your competitors. File your trade names and trademarks for federal and state protection. Learn what's out there about your brand.

2. It's a virtual world, and for your brand to succeed, you need to be digitally visible. As a startup, online advertising is a blessing. Affordable and easily measured. Start with a web site and e-mail, and take it from there. Unless you're a techie, this is an area where you'll need to find a partner. There are plenty of web developers and designers out there. Find one that best matches you and your brand, and delve into the world of online marketing as soon as possible. Don't forget traditional advertising and mobile marketing tactics to enhance your digital plan. If you're an established business, start making the migration to a 360-degree marketing strategy today.

3. Take all of the information you've learned and gathered, and create your marketing plan. If you don't feel comfortable doing it alone, find someone who can help you put a plan in place to help you develop a creative strategy for your brand. Research and discover all the 360-degree marketing tactics your best competitor is using for advertising and communications. Study the messages and the media. And then do it better.

A Real Story

Kathleen Murphy

Meet Kathleen Murphy, born in 1954. Founder and president of MurphyEpson, Inc., a marketing consulting firm. Business owner since 1989.

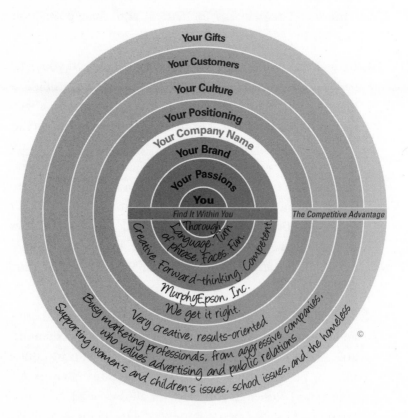

The one word that best describes me is thorough. I try to know as much as I can about the subject I am working on because it helps me come up with fresh ideas. My company's positioning statement is "We get it right"—which is more a state of mind than a marketing slogan. We are a small boutique agency that delivers high quality services to our clients. As an advertising agency, it's imperative for us to guide our clients about all different types of marketing tactics—traditional, digital, and mobile. With the pace of change today, we need to make sure our employees—and me, too—are keeping up, staying ahead.

Our business is very creative and results-oriented. We want to get things done and out the door. The tempo is very fast, with many projects underway simultaneously. If you saw our company on the street, it would be running, not walking. We would look sleek and have a good cardio system. One of the many ways we speak to our clients is through environmental branding. You can feel our culture the second you walk through the door. I chose to share my office space with a design studio, so it's full of whiteboards, comfortable furniture, warm colors— all of which exude an ambiance that this is a place where people think and create out of the box. We take advantage of well-done signage, color, and imagery in our office to help communicate who we are.

If you're just starting out, my tips are to have optimism, organization, and persistence. The most rewarding part about owning your own business is that you can be successful, you can work with other creative people, which is extremely energizing, and you are never bored.

I tell all of my clients a marketing plan is essential. It's my business, but it is at the heart of most businesses as well. Marketing plans don't need to be elaborate, but they do need to be written and understood by key stakeholders. And I firmly believe that documenting return on investment is key. If you

feel like you can't create your own marketing plan, there are
many professionals to turn to for help. It is fun for us in mar-
keting, and it can be for you and your brand, too.

Kathleen's business is marketing, and she knows the importance of a plan. She has one for her own company, and her brand
was articulated clearly from the beginning, because she knew
what she wanted to create and knew she would be her own
boss. And because of her clear definition of her strengths, she has
been able to define a real brand that provides thorough advice
and counsel to hundreds of companies, and she gets it right from
the minute they walk in the door of her office.

RECOMMENDED READING

♦ *Small is the New Big: and 183 Other Riffs, Rants, and*
Remarkable Business Ideas by Seth Godin. This is my
favorite book by this bestselling and prolific author. His
ideas stimulate creativity and open your eyes to the change
all around us. Godin's grasp of the digital world and its
power is key.

Life Lesson Twelve: Make it tangible

As soon as you open an office and a customer walks through the
door, you're a retailer, even if your business is to other businesses
and not consumers. How your office looks, how your employees
dress, and what colors are on the walls are all part of the branding
mix. In marketing jargon, these are called *touch points*—everywhere people come into contact with your real brand. The art
of real branding at its best is when you've addressed all the ways

a customer touches your brand, and they're all in sync, and they're a reflection of you. Your environment brings this all to life.

Today's legendary retailers have it down. Have you walked past an Abercrombie & Fitch store lately? From outside, you can hear the beat of hip—and loud—music. Same thing at Hollister. As you walk inside these stores, you're greeted by a young 20-something wearing merchandise and exhibiting a clear image of the retailers' brand. There are leather couches in groupings, large black and white photos of perfect bodies adorn the walls, and you know from the door whether you are the target audience or not. It's environmental branding at its finest. Every component of the store—from the merchandise, to the displays, to the furnishings, to the employees, to the music—reinforces the brand and is the reason why young people go there in droves to shop. They like the look, the attitude, and the lifestyle it all projects. And they've seen it before, in Hollister's and Abercrombie & Fitch's ads, online, in catalogs and anyplace else these retailers choose to set their brands in motion. Classic retailers such as Neiman Marcus and Nordstrom's have had this down for years. Newer entries like Nike and Apple are wowing consumers with their brand's expression in the retail arena, too, making the store an incredible experience. The Hershey store in Times Square has huge lines of people waiting to enter during peak seasons, even though the drugstore across the street has the same exact candy bars for sale.

Environmental branding has long been a staple in retailing, but now it's cropping up in offices with increasing frequency. Here's why:

Environmental branding reinforces a company's image in the marketplace and helps consumers find them in a vast sea of competition.

Just like a logo or a positioning statement, environmental branding helps solidify your identity and what you provide to your customers. It includes the use of signage, architecture, colors, furnishings, scents, music, and interior design.

For example, when you walk into Real Living's corporate offices, you're surrounded by the color red—lots of it—and round shapes—all visual extensions of our brand. This branding is at work beyond our walls, too, through the creation of an environmental branding program for our residential real estate offices nationwide. When we open a new office, the new broker-owner can select from a suburban, urban, or rural prototype to fit the market and location. We worked with a national retail design firm to create a specific color palette for walls, flooring, and furniture for each of the settings and ideas for matching decorative accents. When a buyer or seller walks into one of our offices, we want them to feel welcome and comfortable—just like they are at home. We have office furniture layouts for the Real Living living room and suggested zones customers can move through as they go from indecisive investigators to clients. These types of retail strategies are key because they let your employees and customers know your brand is consistent. Your office is where your brand is living. Is it right? Is it the real you?

As we've noted, Real Living was built on top of two very traditional real estate companies with traditional cultures. Real estate companies from the 1950s and on changed very little. They modeled their environments after banking—to look serious. The definition of professional was very strict and narrow, modeled on traditional male beliefs that suits, quiet, control, and dark wood means you have substance. Well, needless to say, we had to change the face of real estate from imagery of two men in suits shaking hands in front of a yard sign to lava lamps and smiles. There wasn't a lot of fun or consumer focus in the business, and that's what Real Living was created to bring back. When implemented,

Real Living Prototype Office

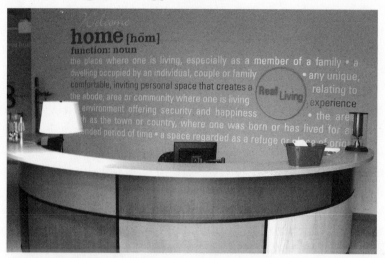

our office environmental branding packages make customers and our agents smile. The environments feel high energy, productive, and infused with our brand words and spirit. Emotion in the office. It's foreign to the way traditional business was operated, but foundational to your real brand.

One of my favorite examples of environmental branding by a retailer is Dylan's Candy Bar in New York City. Walk in there and try to leave without buying something sweet. Giant lollipops, bright colors, and more bring the store to life. And, similarly, visit dylanscandybar.com. You feel like you're in the store. The brand is seamlessly executed online and off.

No matter your size, you are how you look. Your environment is your brand. As an intuitive woman entrepreneur, this element of branding may seem obvious. If not, just remember the five senses, and you'll have a good start. For help, turn to a design firm or environmental design expert. Again, trust is key, and remember you are in charge.

And finally, once you've decided on the look and feel of your physical office space, don't forget that you need to translate that environmental branding to your online office, especially your home page. The online and offline worlds have collided and, as we've already discussed, your brand needs to be a part of both. Online and offline sales and services need to mirror each other. The Internet provides an unrivaled means of getting to know your customers, in real time and on their terms. Beyond the look and feel, you must have relevant, engaging content and a true value proposition, of course. You need to figure out your customer relationship communication and management strategies, which at their foundation are replicating in-person relationships. Not replacing them, but imitating touch points. These online touch points should replicate the interactions in the real world. As much as possible, communicate with your customer as if you were personally speaking with her. Remember, there's no such thing as online customers; just customers. If you are not maximizing your relationships, modeling them, and scaling those findings to your online approach to generate revenue, well, you're missing the boat. At the very basic level, it's about brand.

Beyond the brand standards package—logo, colors, font, imagery—your online office should replicate the environmental feel of your brand. Think of your home page as the front door of your traditional, real, physical office. What that brand definition means online is much the same as offline. We have large lava lamps in our office and lava bubble icons online, to give you a basic example. We paint walls red, and we anchor our site with red. We use inspirational and aspirational words in our office, and online. It's all about bringing your brand to life online. And force yourself to commit to rich media online. Use video to bring your brand to life. Don't do it in the traditional sense: all about you. Nope, shoot a video about your brand and what it makes your customers feel like. Today's consumers want to get to know you and your brand. They want a real, personal connection. Video is a great way to translate your philosophy and brand online. Post it on your site, and then post it on YouTube. Send it by e-mail to new prospects. Think of video as a chance to invite them into your office, virtually.

And here's a final, but important, point: A critical ingredient to a great brand is your brand keeper.

Who is yours? If it's you, make sure you have the bandwidth to police it and grow your business. If not, then assign a chief. Don't delegate to someone outside your business. This is not a job for an advertising agency, no matter what they tell you. This isn't negotiable. We're talking about you and your brand here. For too many years, clients allowed their advertising agencies to take notes and then disappear and create. Thus followed the big presentation where the client would either be wowed or disappointed. Today, all of this must be a collaborative process. And whether your marketing guru is you, a graphic designer, or a bigger team, the key is to keep the essence of the brand with you. So hire your marketing counsel well. Ad agencies make ad campaigns—you make your brand. Brand stewards must reside within your company. Don't settle for just being a client to your ad agency: You need to be a partner. Don't let them forget your essence, but realize you may need help. Advertising can be complex. Find an agency to help pull together a great ad campaign. Just remember, that's not branding, that's advertising. You are the brand.

What you are trying to achieve with your real brand is authenticity throughout your entire organization by bringing your brand to life.

I truly believe vision and creativity, in alignment, are unstoppable.

You, as a business owner, need to create not just a company, not just a brand, but a real brand, online and off. This is the fun part. Enjoy.

QUESTIONS TO THINK ABOUT

1. Do you have a plan for your office? Before you sign a lease, imagine the perfect exterior. Is it downtown or suburban? In a skyscraper or free-standing? Hardwood floors or carpet? Chrome or cherry? Go back to your brand boards and review what exterior and interior design elements mirror you and your brand. Your environment is key. Get yours right.

2. Building your brand online is much the same as offline, except for the different skill sets you'll need to hire. Look at the brand board you created for your real world brand. That's where you'll start to build your brand online. How can you use today's media distribution choices—social networking, blogging, video—to speak to your customers in a unique way and build that emotional, real connection? Does your office environment represent your brand essence and your passions? How about the home page of your web site?

3. Who is your brand keeper? Is it you? Do you need to hire a retail space planner? An interior decorator? An architect? A web architect? A web developer or web designer? An ad agency or a marketing consultant? Do you need a PR firm or a video production company? Will you attempt to hire a person to orchestrate all of these creative teams? If it's you and your computer right now, that's fine. But having a vision for the future, and who and what you will need, is imperative.

ACTION STEPS

1. Design a plan to create your real-world office. If you're overwhelmed by the notion, get help. Ad agencies often have relationships with retail space planners and designers or have experts on staff. This doesn't need to be expensive, by the way. Sometimes, a few cans of paint are all you need. At jumphome.com, the tree frog brand, we hired an artist to paint the walls frog green and found some gigantic artificial lilies to create the pad. When you're extending your brand online or to a new office, bringing your unique

perspective to the world, remember to keep it real. Remember to consider all the senses of branding. Oh, and what's the dress code for your employees? That will convey your brand, too.

2. You need to mirror your environmental branding in your online office. How complex is your real brand? Is your business straightforward—say selling a common item—or is it complex? The Web gives you unlimited space and freedom to sell yourself, to tell your story, but it needs to be compelling. How deep, how many pages will your online office need to be? Will you use an employee or internal intranet site? Will you sell online and be in need of e-commerce applications? Map out all of this. Is your tone serious or fun? Creative or conservative? Those brand essences should result in very different looking web sites.

3. Remember you are your own brand keeper, even with a consultant or two onboard. When interviewing potential marketing partners, make sure they listen to you. Keep it real. And if anyone in the marketing business tries to confuse you with jargon—an all-too-common ploy used especially by media sales folks—find someone else. You want to hire and work with people who understand you and the heart of your real brand. You must be able to trust them with your brand in the world.

A Real Story

Bev Bethge

Meet Bev Bethge, born in 1964. Founder and chief
creative officer of Ologie, a branding company.
Business owner since 1987.

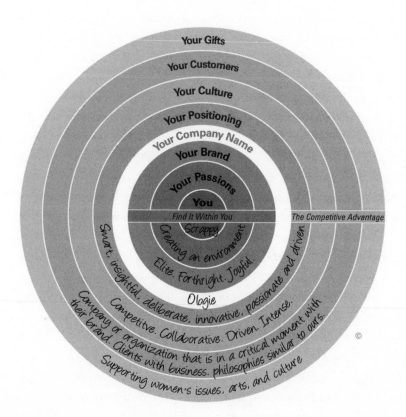

Entrepreneurship is second nature to me. The only time I worked for someone else was when I was scooping ice cream as a teenager. I would be scared to death working for someone else today, because I know I can please myself. I can't imagine going to work and being judged. Right out of college, I founded my first firm. Since then my business has been refined and evolved from pure design to strategic brand management. We're now a leading branding agency with 55 employees called Ologie, which means to study things. And we believe that's what we do: Study people's business, industry, and customer behavior to help them make their brand clear, compelling, and consistent.

I'm nonacademic—an amazing C+ student—and more guttural and street smart with absolutely zero sense of entitlement. I have a keen sense of the environment around me and forecasting—I'm always six months ahead. My passion is creating an environment where great work can happen: Doing my own creative; directing work and making it better; and being allowed to focus on the big picture. Branding is media agnostic. A brand can be expressed in many ways. In the last several years, environmental branding, traditionally reserved for retailers, has evolved to include the work experience.

Our offices are 100 percent ologized. The street entry involves walking through a giant orange O. You've just arrived, and you already know that we are bold. The reception desk is close to the door, and the waiting area is on the other side of the desk—inside our workspace. Now you know that we are welcoming and inclusive. The long open hallway is lined with our philosophy about branding. And the attributes of our people. This is how we tell you that we are smart. The bathrooms are leveraged by having messages on one side of each door and a payoff to that message on the other side of each door. Now you know that we are truly interactive. (And have a sense of humor, too.)

Our work environment works hard at communicating our brand. Yes, it's orange (that's our color)—but it's so much more than that. This not only educates our clients, it reminds our associates of the many ways that they can live the brand on a daily basis. That's powerful!

Bev's own expertise is in marketing, a skill she uses to help her clients—and to build her brand. As a woman entrepreneur in the midst of the changing media and advertising world, Bev has stayed current and kept up. That's a key for entrepreneurs, and it is vitally important for your real brand's marketing efforts. Bev's office environment embraces her personal and real business brand. It bursts with her signature brand color—orange—and resonates with and through each of her employees.

RECOMMENDED READING

♦ *The Brand Gap: How to Bridge the Distance Between Business Strategy and Design* by Marty Neumeier. Just looking through it is stimulating to your creative juices.

In this Real Fact, we completed the fourth layer of the RYI chart, as you filled in your positioning statement. Your brand in the world. We discovered the 360 degrees of marketing in a traditional, digital, and mobile media world, and we highlighted the importance of the five senses of branding. Bringing your brand to life in your real, and virtual, office was the important final life lesson. Once that real office is inhabited by you and your first employee, you're creating a culture. It's best to define it first. That's the focus of Real Fact 5.

Living a life is like constructing a building;
if you start wrong, you'll end wrong.

Maya Angelou

your culture

REAL FACT #5

Create a Unique and Real Work Environment

You are an entrepreneur. You found the drive within you, and you're now working on your competitive edge. One of the most crucial competitive advantages can be a great culture. If you start and develop a work environment that is real, creative, and stimulating, well, you're on your way to huge success. Why? Because just like you, people who work for you want to feel inspired by their jobs. Everybody, at heart, wants to be a part of a team that is building something great, sustainable, worthwhile, memorable, and real. You do. That's why you're an entrepreneur. Entrepreneurs, by definition, are remaking the rules, redefining what business looks, feels, and acts like.

You're also hiring character and personality as much as pedigree. You rightfully ask yourself: Does the potential employee fit the tempo of my company? Culture is the focus of Real Fact 5. How do you define yours, hire to it, and keep it positive? Remember your goals include valuing creativity, expressing your brand in hiring, and avoiding culture vultures. Whether you're hiring one person or a huge team, how do you ensure your brand essence is shared and cared for, respected, and nurtured? Quite possibly, it's simply a matter of finding the right team and then treating it with respect and care. In this Real Fact, I'll offer guidelines to get you started in the right direction as you build or redefine your team. Think of culture as a building process, a vital step in creating your real brand.

In this Real Fact, you'll learn these key life lessons:

♦ Be a creative leader

♦ Express your brand in hiring

♦ Avoid culture vultures

By the end of this Real Fact, you will have filled in the fifth layer of the RYI chart with a definition of your culture.

? Did you know?

After an 11-year research study, Kotter and Heskett found that companies that maintained a positive cultural influence over customers, stockholders and employees did better economically than companies that did not maintain similar positive cultural traits.

Keeping with this trend may increase revenues by an average of 682 percent.

At Real Living, we set out to "change the face of residential real estate." It's an internal rallying cry, putting action to our goal of building "a network of leading real estate companies built on family, innovation, and results." How do we go about changing the face of real estate? It starts with great people, big imaginations, and a very healthy dose of creativity. Change doesn't happen any other way. Take a look at the brand essence in layer three of your RYI chart. How are you going to bring those words to life for your employees? Your culture is just waiting to be born.

Life Lesson Thirteen: Be a creative leader

In Real Fact 4, we talked about the importance of positioning your brand in the world. This Real Fact's life lessons are about making sure each one of your employees is an expression of your real brand. To do that, everyone in your organization needs to understand your brand essence, your external positioning and your vision for the company. And it's not enough just to tell a new employee on the first day. To consciously create a positive work culture of your dreams takes, well, work. It isn't a one-time meeting to roll out an ad campaign. It's about how you act toward everyone who works for you. Do you embody the qualities you are passionate about? (Okay, at least on most days?) Do your employees know the real you, the center of the chart? Do you have a rallying cry, a common vision articulated in action?

That's creative leadership. Think about great leaders. They rally a team through purpose. They are goal driven. Confident. Exuberant. Focused. Great bosses are leaders, not managers. They are willing to make tough decisions and stand by them. This isn't a popularity contest. It's your livelihood. That said, compassion, fairness, understanding, and a look back to your vision should come into play, as well. Powerful passion is key, too.

While leadership does call for skills you may be lacking, such as stepping out front, public speaking, and the like, these capabilities can be learned and fostered over time. If you want to go for it, you can and will. Sometimes the most effective leaders are quietly so. Whatever your style, what sets apart creative leaders from others is that they embody their real brand essence in everything they do and say. Creative leaders don't have one demeanor in the boardroom and another with their assistants. Nope. They are consistent. And real. They dress, speak, and act not in an attempt to fit in, but instead in a style to create their own way. You are uniquely capable of creating the culture and environment you've always dreamed of working within.

> You will draw others to you based on your clarity of vision, your purpose, and your culture.

You are your brand ambassador, its personification, and its biggest recruiting draw. Who do you want to surround yourself with in the office? What type of culture do you want to create and work within? Are you more formal or informal? Do you envision a hierarchical organization or a team? Based on my past experiences, I knew what I didn't want. I also knew I valued the importance of teams and breaking down silos. Unlike most of the bosses in my past, who kept people and departments separated, today's successful companies know silo-busting is key in the interactive age. Integration counts. As we've built Real Living—a new company resting on the shoulders of two 50-year-old real estate firms—we've had our share of struggles merging cultures and integrating. And we've learned a lot about the power of integration. Sales, marketing, training, IT, organizational development, and all the other departments must come together to achieve common goals. Even if it's just a handful of people, they all need to be rowing the boat in the same direction, and it's your job to captain the ship, and, occasionally, grab an oar.

Be innovative about how to connect people on your team. Is it happy hours or cross-department projects, potluck breakfasts, or holiday parties? Perhaps it's as simple as asking for a personal touch base at the start of regularly scheduled meetings. Whatever the answer, it needs to feel natural to you and your style, and it needs to be ritualized. Don't just do something once and think you've built culture. This is a big job, and you're just the leader to do it.

A key strategy we've found to foster communication and teamwork is mixing the physical location of offices—sprinkling some IT folks in with the sales team, for example. Proximity does create understanding, and hopefully, collaboration. We've also worked hard at interdisciplinary accountability groups and team-building exercises. Before you roll your eyes, which I tended to do before I saw these things actually work, understand that I'm not suggesting an Outward Bound–type course for your company, but, quite simply, for you to acknowledge that departmental silos by discipline hold you back; that in the age of the Internet, collaboration is key and sharing is instantaneous. And the more your employees know one another both personally and professionally, the stronger your culture will be. It's all one part of the hallmark of being a great creative leader.

Your real brand deserves a real leader. Someone who inspires others, embraces ideas, takes risks, makes the world a better place, and makes her team work together. This is exciting. You're building a passionate brand, believers who will represent you well and proudly. The people who work at the business, collectively devising a product or service, create real culture. Culture doesn't rise from a sentence written in a boardroom. It emerges when you manage your current associates to live out your vision. Make them part of the process by listening to and adopting their ideas. The speed of the team is the speed of the leader, as they say. Get moving. You're uniquely qualified to do this. Happy employees make happy customers. Show your team the best

Did you know?

Women business owners are more likely than their male counterparts to seek out the opinions and input of others.

Source: NFWBO Study, "1999 Facts on Women-Owned Businesses: Trends in the US and the 50 States"

qualities of a creative leader, and you'll receive the same qualities back in return, as will your customers.

Just remember, as your business grows, it will become crucial to delegate so you can lead. All successful entrepreneurs experience growing pains. If you were capable of doing everything at launch, great. But now your company is larger, so working smarter—not harder—is key. You must trust the team you are building. Give them specific direction and communicate often, but allow them to execute their way. You cannot grow and remain in control of every detail. Entrepreneurs focus only on building their product or service. Leaders trust their team and work patiently to develop their strengths. And they don't micromanage. Leaders grow great businesses by becoming more than their initial idea. They paint the vision of the future and lead the team to it. You will need to become a leader as your business grows. You can do it, and you'll find it feels good to build a culture and create something lasting and much bigger than you. You're making a real difference with your real brand in the world. Your role in your growing Real business is to inspire. It's as simple as that.

QUESTIONS TO THINK ABOUT

1. Are you capable of leading, instead of managing? Do you know the difference?

2. Do you have a good role model for your cultural positioning? A company where you've worked, perhaps, or simply an ideal or a leader you admire? Think of those traits, those behaviors that make that person rock.

3. Can you envision a culture infused with creativity and energy? What does that mean to you?

ACTION STEPS

1. Revisit your brand essence words from the third layer of the RYI chart. Can you put them into an internal call to action for your employees? If not, create a phrase, a rallying point that captures what you envision. Then put it in the next layer—the fifth—of the RYI chart: your culture.

2. If you have employees already, it's time to get them up to speed. You need to present them with your RYI chart—at least the parts you feel comfortable sharing. They need to know your brand essence and why. They need to know what matters to you and why.

3. Consider a business coach to help you with any management issues you feel you have. It is an investment in yourself that can truly pay off for all of those who work for you. Being a great leader takes work, constant reinforcement, and focus. When you think about the future, what type of leader will your business require? Do you have or want to develop those skill sets? If not, can you hire to them?

A Real Story

Judith Wright

Meet Judith Wright, born in 1951. President and
co-founder of The Wright Leadership Institute.
Author of *More* and *The One Decision*. Business
owner since 1984.

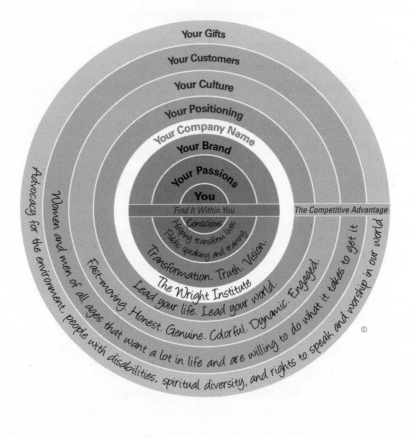

Everything we do at the Wright Leadership Institute helps people not just lead their lives, but the world around them. Our students naturally affect the world, leading others to their highest potential, transforming their families, businesses, organizations, professions, and fields. I love being able to see difference we've made. Leaders are created, not necessarily born. There are leadership skills that everyone can learn to improve upon, and you should continue learning for life. That's the fun part of living.

I don't necessarily think I'm a better leader because I am a woman, but I do know that my feminine strengths give me an advantage. The top three tips I would give to a woman starting her own business are:

1. *Honor your unique feminine gifts.*

2. *It's your business, so design it in a way that reflects who you are, your values, your passion. Create the culture that best personifies you. Create a business that you love working in. And focus on developing your leadership skills as your business grows.*

3. *Have strong, honest support around you. Surround yourself with people who will tell you the truth and give you straight feedback. Form a board or team of successful people as advisers who want you to succeed, and use them well.*

Judith coaches creative leaders as a profession. She helps her clients seize opportunities and define their workplaces uniquely. Her love of speaking and writing—on national television shows or to small groups—allows her to express her values and passion to ever-broader audiences. But first, she had to become a creative leader herself.

RECOMMENDED READING

♦ *Crucial Conversations: Tools for Talking When Stakes are
   High* by Kerry Patterson, Joseph Grenny, Ron McMillan,
   and Al Switzler. One female entrepreneur swears this book
   saved her partnership and their business by forcing dialogue and helping them reopen the lines of communication. It's important, especially as you grow. If you need
   help, give this book a try.

Life Lesson Fourteen: Express your brand in hiring

If you've decided to strive for authenticity and have articulated
your personal and business brand, you're off to a good start. You
know the word that describes you best and the three words that
best represent the company you aspire to build. Those words
become the heart of everything else you do. You are dedicated to
creatively leading, not managing. When it comes time to hire your
first employee—or land your first client—you need to see those
same qualities reflected in your work. It's affirming. It's right.
Being true to yourself is never the wrong choice.

Now that you are five rings into your RYI chart, key words for
job descriptions have emerged. It's interesting how this all works
together, right?

The real fact is that your dreams for your personal brand align
clearly with the vision for your company's future and paint the
path for everything else.

Believe it or not, you can tell a lot about a company from the
job postings on Monster or CareerBuilder, or in the newspaper,
almost as much as you can about a candidate from her resume. So
before the candidates even walk through the door, paint the picture
of the company you're trying to create in your job descriptions.

In Real Fact 2, we covered the snarks, folks who shouldn't be a part of your trusted adviser network, or members of your team. We described how to spot them and what to watch out for. Snark is the opposite of real and most recently traces its roots to the IT industry. Dictionary.com calls it a system failure, or any kind of unexplained event on a computer. Just as I advised you to be on the lookout for snarks who might try to infiltrate any part of your life, I'm now advising you to be particularly wary of them in the workplace because of the negative consequences that might ensue. If you hire too many of these folks, you will have a culture failure. Guaranteed. As soon as you recognize anyone in your company as a snark, let him or her go. If they are not supporting you, they are using you, and they need to exit. Your goal is to build a real, snark-free company filled with honest people who share your values.

Real people are dedicated and believe in you and your culture, and their support helps move the rest of the team along.

Real people respect that it's your company but contribute as if it's theirs. It's a mutual appreciation relationship, 50–50, open, and true. Outside of work, these are your best friends, confidantes, closest advisers, and significant others. At the office, these are the employees you can trust, who give you honest feedback. They are loyal, respectful people you can be yourself around.

Who are they? It varies from business to business, industry to industry. My team at Real Living is heavily weighted with women employees. As long as we're working as a team, that's a wonderful thing. As women, we know women can be our own worst enemies in a pack, but our best friends individually. If we can wrangle the good from one another, support one another collectively *and* individually, imagine the power.

As you build your brand and your business, hire carefully. Sometimes you don't see problematic employees coming. A couple of recent examples should illuminate whom you shouldn't hire. As I began hiring for Real Living, building a startup company on top of existing companies, the first hires were key. My very first choice was a go-getter former employee. She was everything I knew my new brand needed: passionate, energetic, committed, driven, and she had my back. During the integration of companies and the shake-up of old and new, she was my eyes and ears and single-mindedly supporter. She treated me with respect and encouraged me every step of the way. I thought, as we built our team, she would be a creative leader of others. Unfortunately, I'd hired an Ego Snark.

Her passion and drive—misused—drove a wedge between her and every other member of the Real Living team. Single-mindedness without open-mindedness is lethal. Soon other department heads were complaining. It became a chorus of grievances against her: disrespecting others' opinions and meddling in other people's business, especially, became big problems. Instead of doing her work, she was micromanaging others in our growing team, while alienating most co-workers. As her boss, I found watching this self-destructive transpiration disheartening. A great talent was being wasted and, in the end, for the good of the whole meant she had to move on. The damage to my reputation and general morale was reparable, but it took time. When you hire and keep around an Ego Snark, it reflects poorly on you.

Another hire, who turned out to be a Con Artist Snark, caused a bigger setback. Again, we didn't see it coming. This employee is close to an Ego Snark, but she didn't have the skill set to be completely dangerous. Qualities of a Con Artist Snark include a complete lack of transparency and accountability. The employee took credit for other people's ideas, replete with an extensive resume packed full of milestones she did not meet. Using the good old boys' network to her full advantage, she used the fact of being a woman to become the token on boards and the like, but she never turned back to lend a hand to another woman. All show and no substance, she wowed us with her seeming sophistication and smooth presentation skills. It took too long to find out her contributions would consist entirely of schmoozing, draining expense accounts, and taking credit for everyone else's accomplishments wherever she could gain access to a microphone.

Then there are hires who aren't snarks, but who just don't click in your workplace. And this goes without saying, no matter how nice an employee is, bottom line, you have to expect performance—and they have to be real and offer your business more than what you've invested in them. That's the nature of work. You should expect nothing less.

As we've grown and attempted to keep defining our culture along the way, we look for those who display energy, enthusiasm, and who have done their research on our values. As I described in Real Fact 3, our company's brand essence is family, innovation, and results. It's articulated through the key words: round, red, and real. We're trying to create a snark-free company filled with transparency and accountability. A place filled with motivated folks who don't expect a lot of—or any, really—micromanaging. A place free of back-hall, back-room discussions. No ulterior motives. No artificial hierarchy where things happen because they've always been that way. And, you probably guessed it, a very casual dress code. We have a Ping-Pong table in the lobby, which sets the tone of our work environment.

People get us or they don't. It's okay. We aren't a good fit for everyone, but we are, hopefully, just perfect for the right ones.

Recently, a young woman interviewed for a position in marketing. Spunky and exuding confidence, I thought she would be a great fit. The marketing director, who would be her direct supervisor in the position, didn't agree, and the offer wasn't extended. See, no micromanaging. The young woman followed up with a note to me, saying: "I'm going to get hired for a job here. It's where I want to work. I love the environment, the people, the feeling I get when I walk in the door. I'm going to keep trying until you hire me." I love that. Her personal brand is—even in her early

20s—quite defined. She knows what she wants and what she's looking for in her first job out of college. I'm sure she'll find a spot, with us, or an even better cultural fit.

When you're building your team, take the time to find the person who will reflect your values, support you, and be there when needed. You want to have a balance of personalities. Your computer programmers could be your total opposite, but you have to know they are true, real, and reliable. I move fast and over-whelm people who can't keep up. That's not to say, when I look around the room at Real Living, that everyone reflects that quality. We would all be a hyper mess. Some people reflect the real, genu-ine, and peaceful aspect of the company. Others demonstrate the family histories of our firm. All of us are focused on results though, because you really can't build a fast-growing company without innovation and results. Up front, communicate your culture, essence, and what you're all about. Put it in writing in a job description. Talk about it during the interview process. You might scare off some potential people. It's not foolproof, but at least it gives them a heads-up about what's in store. Also try to get poten-tial hires to talk about themselves. You can get a good read on a person in the first few minutes of dialogue. Real can't be faked.

And of course, building a team is much more than just the right personality. You are looking for the best talent you can find for the position. Do background checks. Call references. Avoid HR people if possible, and go to direct supervisors. In today's litigious society, it's sometimes tough to get an honest reference. But some-times the less said about a potential candidate can be telling. If you keep hearing comments such as, "Dave worked here from January 2002 to March 2004," and nothing else, that's probably a red flag. I recall a recent person we interviewed for a sales position. On paper and in the initial interview, we liked what we saw. Our impression changed when we called her references. Companies typically want to help eliminate snarks from the workplace. Most companies don't wish a bad employee on another company.

Make interviewing a collaborative process and involve your team. Our prospective hires meet with people from various departments, not just those whom they'll work the most closely with. Soliciting input from your team will help you determine who is and isn't a good fit. It's also an empowerment builder for your team to take ownership of the hiring process. Some people may think you end up with too much information going this route, but, in my opinion, it's the only way to hire.

QUESTIONS TO THINK ABOUT

1. If you're planning to make a new hire soon, take time to think about job descriptions and postings. What should they say to communicate what you're looking for?

2. What key words could you use in your hiring and interview process to explain the culture you're trying to create to a candidate?

3. How will you handle the hiring process? Will you handle it alone? With employees come human resources issues. Do you have a good handle on benefits and the like, or will you need help?

ACTION STEPS

1. As you begin to build or expand your team, create job postings that give an inside look at your culture. Not too much, but enough that some candidates get it before they walk in the door.

2. During the interview process, build on the job description by sharing your culture, essence with potential candidates, and clearly explaining your expectations. And don't forget to involve other members of your team.

3. If you don't plan to hire in-house HR capabilities, be sure you have a means to outsource all of the benefits and legal work involved with having employees. HR outsourcing is on the rise and can be a great resource for growing entities.

A Real Story

Sue Chen

Meet Sue Chen, born in 1970, is president, CEO and CFO of Nova Ortho-Med, Inc., a manufacturer of mobility, patient aid, and bathroom safety products. Business owner since 1993.

I started my company right after college, and that came with many challenges. One of them was creating a great culture with trustworthy, energetic and loyal employees—the key to a successful business.

I'm very upfront with candidates and new hires about expectations. Every new employee goes through a one-on-one orientation with me. I make sure he or she understands all aspects of the company including profitability, expenses, sales, and their direct impact and contribution to the company. And all of our employees know who our customer is and what their expectations are. We know we must always be ready for what comes our way and be prepared to do it better. The only way to get bigger and better is to take on bigger and better. My employees are always ready and anxious for the next challenge.

I'm a firm believer in no office politics. No bureaucracy. No closed-door policy. If you have to come to work, it should be fun and productive. Our environment is very positive, fast paced, and downright scrappy. It's also very entrepreneurial—each employee really cares about Nova and its success. It's so rewarding to see someone's evolution. To see their maturity and growth as they embrace the company like it's their own. We have 40 employees and two locations, Los Angeles and Chicago. I have different hiring methods for each job type and very specific job descriptions. For some positions, we use an outside agency and require that potential hires go through the agency for three months so we can monitor their work ethic and how they get along with others before we hire them directly. For others, I use employment web sites and industry referrals. When interviewing, I especially look for integrity, a strong work ethic, and a positive attitude.

My current executive team earned their roles through longevity, loyalty, and commitment.

I don't think I'm a better boss because I'm a woman, but I do think strong communication skills are essential to being an

effective leader. That means you can both listen well and express
expectations, praise, criticism, and motivation.

When it comes to hiring and retaining employees, Sue has it
all figured out. She knows what it takes to succeed in her demanding business. The connection and partnership she fosters in her
firm is the stuff that successful businesses are made of.

Recommended Reading

♦ *How to Run Your Business Like a Girl: Successful Strate-*
  gies from Entrepreneurial Women Who Made It Happen
  by Elizabeth Cogswell Baskin.

Life Lesson Fifteen: Avoid culture vultures

Even if you stay true to all of the circles in your RYI chart, as well as
your instincts, you will encounter culture vultures. Maybe because
the more fulfilled and empowered you become, the more attractive
you are to circling vultures—I'm not sure. What I am sure about is
that you will encounter these human roadblocks I call *culture vul-*
tures along the way. You know who I'm talking about—the nonteam
players, the ones who lay down the sandbags for roadblocks, challenge change agents, and can't think out of the box.

Unlike snarks or employees who just don't fit in the culture,
these folks operate at a higher level and are more difficult to see
and eliminate. They have power, and they use it against you daily.
Perhaps your vulture takes the form of a legacy employee who
knows the backstory of the company you've acquired. You need
that legacy knowledge transfer, but all the while, you must realize

what that is costing you and your culture. You are stuck with the employee, for the time being. There may be more than one vulture, depending on the size of your business. Be on guard. The moment you suspect you don't have someone's 100 percent commitment, you're right. Intuition is a gift, and you should listen to it. If you're starting a business from scratch, you need to watch out and not create or keep a culture vulture any longer than you must.

> If you've purchased an existing business, like we did with the creation of the Real Living brand, chances are you'll most likely acquire a culture vulture.

They will come in the form of leaders who support you to your face and sabotage you behind your back. Or it's the brandits, as I call them, who undermine your brand's positioning or imagery or strategies you're trying to create. They will be the people in the meeting who roll their eyes at your new idea, but act as if they love it. Some vultures are more overt: openly challenging you and your plans and dreams. The key to remember is you can and will overcome these folks. But the first step is realization. It's hard not to be liked, not supported. To realize that is happening in your own company, when you're working so hard to be real, to be authentic, is tough. I know. The second step is making sure you come out the winner in this power struggle. Shedding light on malcontents sometimes makes them leave, other times it makes them dig in even harder. If you find yourself in that position, stay strong. Confront misinformation as soon as you hear it. Make your network stronger than the vulture's. The truth eventually will come out, because culture vultures reap what they sow. It just doesn't usually happen in the timeframe you're hoping for.

Some of the worst culture vulture experiences occur within family businesses. It typically begins when the second generation has to share the power or when siblings are in business together without clearly defined roles and responsibilities. Feelings get hurt. Mistrust begins and the vulture is circling, waiting to bring the culture down. If you're stuck in this situation, get help. There are plenty of business consultants out there to help you plan a strategy. Sometimes an outsider is what you need to bring fresh perspective. It's hard when you're too close to the situation. But you are stronger than you think, and your dreams are too important to have someone else rain on your parade.

With the goal of getting to know one another better post-merger at Real Living, we hired a consulting firm—actually, several along the way—to bring our disparate leadership team together. We needed help in a big way. The merger didn't start off well at all. Here's why: The people who were dead-set against the brand Real Living were given equal say at all of the accountability group meetings. They weren't held accountable for understanding or supporting the new brand but instead were coddled and made to feel more important. When a facilitator demanded honesty from those around the room, the culture vultures would tell trite tales from their past with no emotional connection while those who were embracing the brand and the process bared their souls. To say this was frustrating would be an understatement. To say it was a waste of time is obvious. With a vulture in the room, honesty and culture suffer. To build culture, you must have alignment. We didn't from Day One. It was part denial and part wishful thinking. If we had dug a little deeper, we may have seen it coming early on. But the important point is, we fixed it. It's a critical lesson: If there are culture vultures in close, powerful positions, they will bring you down unless you neutralize them.

It's a gut-check time again. What is the true cost of keeping someone employed in your company? Beyond salary and benefits, I mean. It's the cost to the team as a whole. Culture vultures are saboteurs. They are dangerous and need to be dealt with. You can't look to the future if you allow an environment where everyone is rowing in different directions. Trust me. You'll see it once you take action. Accountability to one another, as a team, cannot happen unless everyone on the team buys in.

When you work on your culture, with purpose and vision, you will uncover the vultures. Once you do, don't be passive. Don't get used. And as soon as possible, try to remove them from your team. If you can't, proceed with caution and get help.

At Real Living, as our team changes and grows, we learn. You will, too. Every person you hire won't work out, but that's life. When you realize you've made a bad hire, eliminate, sooner rather than later, those who don't fit. We look for a cultural fit from the start. But as our company has grown and changed, we needed different skill sets and different mixes of talent. People evolve, too. The days of having the same job for 40 years is history, and really, that's for the best. You're an innovator, and you need to surround yourself with people who embrace change.

QUESTIONS TO THINK ABOUT

1. If you're already in business, are you employing any culture vultures?

2. Would you be willing to sever a family tie or a friendship if someone was sabotaging you and your business?

3. As you step into your own, as a businesswoman and a powerhouse, are you ready for the roadblocks that are going to come your way? Unfortunately, the more powerfully real you become, the more uncomfortable the vultures become.

ACTION STEPS

1. Be on the lookout for anyone in your company who makes you doubt your vision of your Real brand. There will be enough doubters on the outside.

2. When possible, eliminate culture vultures upon discovery, or as soon as you can. If you need help, hire a counselor or consultant.

3. Hire positive, change-oriented people into your company. Almost every traditional industry has faced or is facing massive changes. It is the way of the world.

A Real Story

Kathy Eshelman

Meet Kathy Eshelman, founder and president of Grade A Notes, a lecture note and publishing service for students and professors. Business owner since 1987.

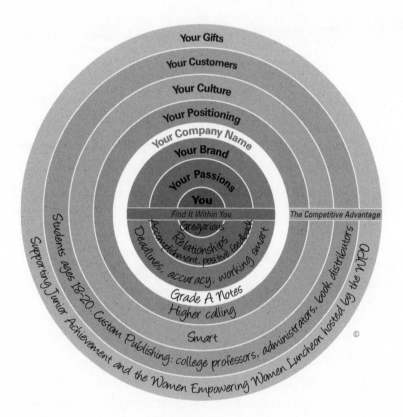

I trace my entrepreneurial roots to age 13 when I was an Avon lady. I also worked as a restaurant waitress, grocery store cashier, and in sales for a direct marketing and printing company. Deadlines, accuracy, and working smart are requirements for my business, which I liken to having a smart, organized college professor by your side. When it came to selecting a name for my business, I hit the dictionary and looked for words that described the operation, its quality, and its higher calling. That's how I came up with Grade A Notes.

I have 12 employees; six of them full time. We hire people who are interested in our business, but don't necessarily have a background in what we do. We believe we can train people to work in our environment. We are more interested in their desire to be a part of our organization than their experience. We like to hire students who live on our street— we're located in the heart of a college campus—as our part-time employees—or friends of our student employees. We have found this to be very effective. Hiring students as employees makes perfect sense for us, because students are our customers. The most important quality we hire to is enthusiasm. I'm proud to say the most rewarding part of owning my own business is employing people and empowering them to follow their own dreams, whether it be within the business or in their personal lives.

It's critically important to have written job descriptions and update them periodically. Those descriptions should be reviewed at an employee's annual review. Over the years, I've found that when job expectations are put in writing, it clears up most of the ambiguity of our expectations.

Empowerment to the staff is my motto. But sometimes empowerment can backfire. I'm not sure I've hired culture vultures, but I've definitely employed a few snarks over the years. The thing is, they're almost unavoidable, and a lot of them you can't recognize until they're already working for you. They gain power and then, wham, you realize what you've got on your hands.

If you're contemplating following my path, my best advice is to follow your powerful intuition—your gut feeling is probably right. I would also encourage you to take charge of your life and its situations. Don't be a victim!

Who wouldn't want to have a boss like Kathy? Her hiring strategies—including hiring her target audience—are smart marketing moves and good steps toward keeping culture vultures away. But, even with all of those hiring measures in place, it's good to be assertive and have a culture vulture elimination plan in place.

RECOMMENDED READING

- ◆ *Never Eat Alone: and Other Secrets to Success, One Relationship at a Time* by Keith Ferrazzi is a great book with powerful networking ideas. His view of people and connections is insightful.

- ◆ Another insightful book is *Smart Women and Small Business: How to Make the Leap from Corporate Careers to the Right Small Enterprise* by Ginny Wilmerding. She explores purchasing a business and working to change the culture. This is a great way to own your own business, but it does offer a different set of challenges and rewards.

In this Real Fact, you learned the essential and powerful truths about culture. Now it's up to you to be the leader of your company and to bring the vision of your brand and its essence to life every day. You need to paint the picture of your real brand in the job descriptions you post, in the way you interview, and in your hiring principles. Be diverse—don't hire a bunch of people just like you, but do hire for passion, commitment, and energy.

And finally, expect that you will encounter snarks and culture vultures. Deal with them expediently.

Congratulations, you've traveled through five layers of the RYI chart! In this Real Fact, you've covered the following:

♦ Be a creative leader

♦ Express your brand in hiring

♦ Avoid culture vultures

In the next Real Fact, we'll tackle your target audience, who may be closer to you than you think.

Just trust yourself. Then you will know how to live.

Goethe

your customers

REAL FACT #6

Your Personal Brand Is
Your Business Brand

You've learned that putting the real you in your business is the essential ingredient for success and happiness, authenticity, and personal validation. You've also embraced the notion that your employees need to understand, feel, and believe in your culture, in you, and your business vision. But there's another audience that needs to feel the real you in your business, and that's your customers.

Throughout this Real Fact, we'll refer to your customers as women. This throws some off, but it shouldn't. By the middle of this century, women will control two-thirds of the wealth in the United States. Comprising more than half of the population and controlling 85 percent of consumer purchases (even higher in some categories), women are, most likely, your customers. Just as you are savvy, creative, and intuitive, so are they.

If you and your brand aren't in sync, these customers know you're faking it.

To reach these women, you need to be everywhere—online, offline, and accessible.

Of course, if your business's target audience is men, or an even mix of men and women, you'll need to accommodate men's needs and wants. However, studies show that if you satisfy a male consumer, you may not even come close to satisfying the female consumer. Satisfy the woman's expectations, and the male customers will be happy, too. When I speak to our company's agents and broker-owners, I refer to our customers as *she* or *her* and by now, they're used to it. I do it purposely, and to make a point. Single women comprise 22 percent of the homebuying market (according to the National Association of Realtors), a number that continues to rise. In fact, after married couples, single women are the largest percentage of homebuyers. When I remind our agents—60 percent of whom are women—they nod in acknowledgment. It's not that we don't welcome and support male homebuyers. Of course we do. The point is when we're marketing, we are marketing to our best customers, the majority of our customers: women.

The purchasing power chart illustrates just some of the categories where women make the majority of purchases, and there are many more. That said, it may seem easy to think you, as a woman, can make sure your business speaks to women. But customizing your business's product or service is essential today, and that means defining your exact customers within a broad target market such as women. Women, as a group, aren't a niche or target audience. We are 51 percent of the population, and that is, after all, a majority. But we cannot be lumped together that broadly in the era of customization. Because, as you and I both know, all women are not the same. While many women entrepreneurs build a business based on

Women's Purchasing Power

Women:

 Make more than 50 percent of all auto purchases and influence 85 percent

 Account for 66 percent of all home computer purchases

 Hold 89 percent of all bank accounts

 Purchase approximately 81 percent of riding lawn mowers

 Make 80 percent of healthcare decisions and account for 67 percent of spending

 Carry 76 million credit cards, 8 million more than men

 Buy not only consumer products and services, but also in the corporate and small business areas

Sources: *2005 Wow! Quick Facts, U.S. Census Bureau, 2004, and Fast Company, 2004.*

a need they perceive in the marketplace for a product or service for people just like them—other women—others pursue businesses with customers who are the opposite. Micromarketing, customization, and niche marketing are the future. So if your audience is women, you better define her a bit more clearly to reach her heart and meet her needs.

And, as we'll discuss later in this Real Fact, even once you've defined your market, you need to constantly change and update your customer segments and profiles. Change is, as we've said repeatedly, the fact of life today. Many established companies just don't understand this. You, as a Real You Incorporated entrepreneur, do. Here's a story to illustrate what your company cannot be. I recently interviewed a woman for a position with our company. The reason why she was looking for a position was that the department she worked for at her previous company—"the department of culture and change"—had been eliminated. "It was a very small department," she explained, adding further that once the mergers were complete, company officials decided the department, and her job, were no longer necessary.

How could a visionary real company create or do away with the department of culture and change? Change is everywhere. It's the one constant that never stops. If her company had the foresight to create this department, it seems logical that eliminating it simply takes the company backward. Change and culture are constant, not a small department to be eliminated. You are the department of change and culture for your Real You Incorporated business. Because if you aren't constantly changing and growing, and your business isn't changing and growing, you're falling behind. Everyone who works for you needs to get comfortable with that notion real fast. Those are the facts today.

Your customers, no matter who they are, demand constant improvement, and they want to help you create it. At the heart of this Real Fact is the notion that you and your business are assessing, evaluating, testing the waters, changing, and genuinely asking your customers to participate every step of the way. Your department of culture and change, whether it is just you or your marketing team—formalized or not—must keep you nimble, flexible, visionary, and innovative, to keep up with customer needs and desires.

The way you express yourself to your customer is beyond advertising and is essential to this circle of the RYI chart. How do you want your customers to feel about their experience with your business? That's what this Real Fact is about—defining a genuine customer experience. And to help you do that, these are the life lessons:

♦ Customers know if you're faking it

♦ Be everywhere she wants you to be

♦ The real world is online

Life Lesson Sixteen: Customers know if you're faking it

Let's face it. You know a fake when you see one. A fake designer purse, an artificial flower, a false friend. You are no different when it comes time to make a purchase. You know when a company isn't what it seems. They may get you the first time, but you won't be back. Now that you're a Real You Incorporated business, it's crucial that you never fake it because your customers will find out. Be true to yourself, and understand enough about your customers to convey your true worth to them at every transaction point.

When I joined a national home services firm in the early 1990s as a marketing executive, I had my hands full. As excited as I was for the opportunity, the man who hired me toured me past a huge office with a big window and real furniture (when I had been accustomed to cubicles at the ad agency), and offered a real salary. But reality set in quickly, as I realized the disparity between our customers and the company's culture.

The profile of a our customer was a woman living in a high-end home, yet the advertisements featured muscle-bound macho men and headlines such as "Call the Mud Wrestlers." Now really, do I want a date with a macho guy when I call, or do I just want cleaning services? Meanwhile, down in the training department, the trainers were teaching the 18-year-old service providers to shake hands with the customer when she opened the door. Like a business meeting. I couldn't help but think, no, I just want you to come in, be respectful, and do your job. It wasn't a handshake business meeting. The young guys knew they were faking it, too. Not only did they feel disingenuous trying to shake a customer's hand, but they quickly realized it made the customer uncomfortable.

To help this business's franchise owners understand the profile of these female customers, I made two sets of art boards and collages packed with photos. One board represented our typical male franchise owner's profile. The other, our female customers. Male business owners and service providers interacting with predominantly wealthy women home-owners. Mostly upper middle class versus mostly working class. You get the idea. While the company had a scalable business model and had been revolutionary in many ways, there was a huge disconnect between internal folks and the external customers. And the more the guys at the company talked to themselves and not to the customers, the bigger the schism.

I've watched in the years since I left as they've fluctuated in their marketing messaging. Customer-focused for a while—testimonials from female customers—and then back to macho images and bad boy humor spots to appeal to their own sensibilities. It's a battle many companies fight. In this case, it's more natural for the powers that be to create and support advertising that speaks to them. If this is your challenge, in the reverse—that your business primarily serves a male customer base—then you, like those guys, must push yourself to understand how men think. Ultimately, it's a learning process. There are huge conferences across the country trying to help companies understand how to market to women, children, gays, seniors, men—you name the market or the niche. Because if you don't understand how to reach your customer, in the right way, they'll know you're faking it. Take notice of the advertising from other industries that targets your customer segment. Notice the common themes, words, and visuals. It will help you crystallize your positioning. And, of course, talk to your customers and ask them.

If you are, like the majority of businesses today, marketing to a female customer base, you, as a woman entrepreneur, are uniquely up to the task. Most important, you are a woman, so you know how we think. You have a leg up, but you still need to do your homework. Marti Barletta's, *Marketing to Women* and *Prime Time Women* are excellent, groundbreaking books about how to market correctly to women. Her books are helpful for all small business owners, whether your venture is B to B or B to C. Right now, you're creating a business around yourself. When it comes time to go to market, the core values in the first section of the chart must shine through. So what do women—your customers—want? Well, a lot. And if you make them happy, your male customers will be, too. We are the demanding ones, as you and I both know. But because we are demanding, we reward excellent experiences by becoming raving fans and spreading the word. We women, with our valuable social networks of friends, family, and colleagues, can do more to help spread the word about a positive customer experience than anybody else. Cross us, talk down to us, be disingenuous, or sexist, and we know it. And we let everyone else in our circle know it, too.

? Did you know?

Eighty-six percent of female entrepreneurs use the same products and services at home as in their business.

Source: Center for Women's Business Research, 2004.

Women entrepreneurs entering fields traditionally dominated by male owners—technology, scientific, and technical services— face a large number of challenges breaking in, but are especially adept at changing the focus of the marketing to reach out to women consumers, be they B to B or B to C. And while the number of women-owned businesses in these categories is still woefully low, the exciting fact to note is that female ownership in these industries has grown 82.7 percent from 1997 to 2006, according to the Center for Women's Business Research. I'm almost certain that you, like me, have had a terrible car dealer- ship experience. It has become clichéd. The lack of respect, attention, and whatever for female customers is legendary. But here's the good news: According to CNW Marketing Research and the National Automobile Dealers' Association, 7 percent of the United States's 20,000 franchised new vehicle dealerships are owned by women, up from 2.9 percent in 1990, and 5.9 percent in 2000. These women trailblazers are changing the customer experience, one dealership at a time. And the numbers reflect an encouraging growth trend. Considering women purchase or have a say in 85 percent of all automobile purchases, we should see these numbers growing rapidly.

With this growth in ownership—in automotive and the other typically male-dominated business areas—women entrepreneurs, like you, will change the way customer service is handled. These businesses will watch their female-owned contemporaries, and they will change. They must. They will become more real, more balanced. More genuine in the treatment of women customers. They will care more about the culture of their businesses, and they will hire happy, non-ego centric people. Not culture vultures, but real, authentic people. Women business owners know this: The happier the employee, the happier your bottom line. In fact, according to a joint study by Bowling Green and Penn State professors Patricia Barger and Alicia Grandey, it could be as simple as a smile. The professors followed 173 encounters between customers and employees in coffee shops, scoring the employees' "smile strength" on a scale from "absent" to "maxi-mal" (which features exposed teeth) at various points during the transaction. The bigger the employee's smile, the more likely customers were to view that person as competent and the encounter—averaging just two minutes—as satisfying.

That said, whether your Real You Incorporated business tackles wholesale trade, utilities, or forestry, your interpretation of customer service and your definition of your customer and customer service will be unique even if you are in the 69 percent of all women-owned businesses that are in the services industry. You also will have a unique, real offering, no matter the competition. That's what it is all about. Creating a business that is real to you—and therefore, becomes real and unique to an ever-growing customer base and filling your employee ranks with people who know and express the real you to the customers.

According to Carolyn R. Pool's Educational Leadership study, published in 1997, emotional intelligence predicts about 80 percent of a person's success in life. We make a majority of our decisions—in business and life—because of emotion. Both men and women. That's why you must understand and build deep, real relationships with your customers. You're creating connections, built on consumer participation and creativity and win your share of heart. In the golden days of media, when broadcast television was king, success was defined by share of voice. But today, it is about share of heart. Every customer is a market.

> So when you bring your Real You Incorporated brand to the world, make it something someone in particular will love, not something that will drive people away. Don't water down your messages to play it safe, or you'll feel like a phony and your customers will sense it, too. Go for something strong, something that's a real representation of you and your brand. People are drawn to a unique point of view. As long as you can back it up. And you can.

This is the circle layer where you're unifying your brand experience—you and your business as one.

To succeed in your business, you are or will soon be a visionary and dynamic leader, and that attracts a loyal cult-like employee following. It's now time to take your offering to the world. You know your competition, and you know why you're better. You've done your homework, and you know your target audience. Who is she? What does she need, and what can you provide? Talk to her in a real way, and she'll be your customer for life. Think about how she will summarize the experience of working with you and your company. And write it on your chart.

QUESTIONS TO THINK ABOUT

1. Are you considering, or have you implemented, business processes that seem disingenuous or fake? Stop it. Just because everybody else says you should do things a certain way doesn't mean you should. If it doesn't feel right to

you, change it. Make sure your business is organized around your customers and her needs.

2. Reflect on your RYI chart. With five layers completed, you have a great picture of what it means to be you in business. Can you articulate your true differentiation? How will you express it to your customers?

3. When your customer completes a transaction or purchase with you, what will she say to her friends? Will it be positively memorable?

ACTION STEPS

1. In your RYI chart, write up to three words about what you would like your customers to feel after working with your company. At Real Living, during and after the transaction, we want our customers to feel at home. Those words, of course, have a double meaning at our company as we help customers buy and sell homes, but your goals could be similar for your customer experience.

2. Implement a customer satisfaction system. Feedback is vital in business. This can be a simple question: Would you refer my business to family or a friend? Or, you can use elaborate feedback forms. Whatever your choice, ask for feedback, and see whether your goal for customer experience is reflected in her words back to you.

3. Set up an established time each month or each quarter for you or your team, if you have one, to touch base with your customers. What's working? What's not? What's changed? What could you do differently or better? If your goal is to stay one step ahead of her—and it should be—you can't sit still.

A Real Story

Tara-Nicholle Nelson

Meet Tara-Nicholle Nelson, born in 1975, owner of *Prosperity Way Knowledge Systems* and www.REThinkRealEstate.com, and author of *The Savvy Woman's Guide to Real Estate*. Business owner since 1997.

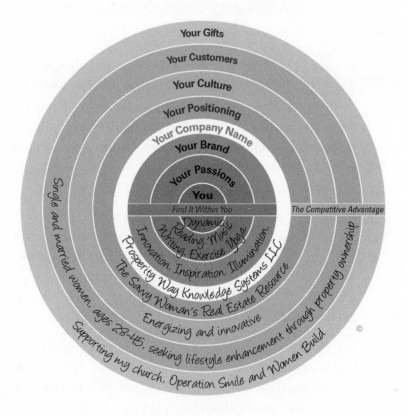

I wanted to control my own destiny; that's why I started my own business. I wanted to create models and platforms that I thought were lacking in the marketplace, but definitely were in demand. I wanted to be able to decide how to spend the precious moments of my life (and time with my family), and to devote those moments to building an asset for my family, rather than for someone else.

My company's culture is all about energy and innovation, of new solutions to age-old problems, some of which are problems of mindset. My customers, women who are seeking lifestyle enhancement though property ownership, whether it be buying, selling, investing in, or remodeling homes, are in the 28 to 45 age range, but we are increasingly seeing women much older than this expressing an interest in our products and in smart property ownership. The aim of my life's work is to create women homeowners.

I know a customer is satisfied when I help her see the reality of homeownership, so I've tried to take the time to know and understand my customer, what she wants, what she needs to accomplish her goals. It's exciting to have the ability to create, to manifest my vision of changing women's lives and turn it into reality. And the most rewarding part of being in this business is when I have a customer who calls or writes and tells me she and her family get to live in their dream home because of my work. That's an amazing feeling.

Tara's business literally is helping women become homeowners. Her ability to help a client find a home—even when her client doesn't believe she can—is an empowering process that leads to great customer satisfaction and business success. The sixth layer in her RYI chart is: Helping women live *in* their dream. What's yours?

♦ *Winning the Toughest Customer: The Essential Guide to Selling to Women*, by Delia Passi and A.B. Aaronson, takes you into the nitty gritty of what she loves, hates, and desires and how to deliver the perfect experience.

Life Lesson Seventeen: Be everywhere she wants you to be

Okay, you want to be everywhere for your customers, talking to her when and how she wants you to be. But how do you do that? Officially, it's called CRM (Customer Relationship Management), and it is crucial because it's about building customer relationships. But don't let the term worry you, because CRM doesn't need to be fancy. Start with defining your best customers, and then segment them into groups, based on behavior and demographics. Make sure, along the way, your customer groups are large enough to warrant your time and a budget. Typically, for any business, there are natural groups of loyal customers, each with unique buying patterns. At Real Living, we knew women were our target audience. But beyond that, we needed to define specific customer types, called segmenting, for CRM. We asked ourselves these questions, and you should, too:

♦ Who are, or will be, my best customers?

♦ What percentage of sales do they or will they generate?

♦ What is their future buying potential?

♦ What is the frequency of purchase?

♦ Why do they or will they pick my company?

From the beginning, Real Living knew our female customers were in the driver's seat. To answer these questions, for us, our broadly defined media-buying target was women ages 25 and above, with household incomes at the top of their markets, who enjoy a full-service real estate experience. We believe up-branding is here to stay, the notion that today's consumers respond to and respect brands with a different, upscale appeal. When we created the industry's first, rich media customer login site at Real Living, MyRealLiving, we did so with her in mind. The site is for customers only, but not just the broad segment mentioned here. We love

Blueprint Buyer

aspirational marketing, messaging, and services that also appeal to customers who will one day be just like our current best customers.

Oh, and because our broker owners and sales agents are our customers too,—we've created a robust intranet site just for them, called the Business Center. There is communication between the two portals, but only at the customer's request. She's in the driver's seat. It's a portal just for her. Once there, our customers can save searches, share information with friends and family, take quizzes, and answer questionnaires to help them get information and much more. The experience changes and grows based on information she shares with us that helps our agents determine which of our customer profile segments she fits in to.

At Real Living, since we're in real estate, we've further segmented our customers by behavior: homebuyers and sellers as well as by age, psychographics, lifestyle, and the like. We've added descriptions, photos, and imagery to accompany each customer type and then created a full series of multimedia advertising campaigns and communications to accommodate each proprietary type. In the following, I've outlined some of our customer segments (based on our own research, in collaboration with interactive agency AKQA, and a number of other sources). While these segments are broad, and we've continued to add refinements, hopefully, these brand boards will be idea starters for your own customer segmentation:

Blueprint buyers are consumers interested in building and designing their own home or moving into a newly constructed home.

Nationally, the share of new homes purchased has remained at slightly more than 20 percent for a number of years.

Blueprint buyers are typically 35 to 54 years old and on average, these buyers spend around $250,000 for their newly built home.

High-End Hunt Club

These buyers are very excited about being the first to live in their new home, and they want plenty of decorating and design ideas. For a special touch, give your clients a few magazines to help get them started, like *Real Simple* and *Domino*.

Unlike most buyers, the high-end hunt club buyers are those looking for homes in the top 10 percent of an area's prices. These buyers also may be in the market for a second home. These are the Prime-Time Women, ages 50 to 70, as defined by Marti Barletta in her book by the same title. These women control the wealth in the United States, and they are a force all businesses should cater to.

The average age of buyers who purchase a second home is 52.

Compared with all buyers who purchase a primary residence— both first-time and repeat buyers-second-home buyers— income is

Savvy Seller

higher. These buyers are most likely to do major renovations to their new home. An agent will need to be up-to-speed on the latest in kitchen, bathroom, and other design trends. Make sure you have trusted contractors and interior designers to recommend.

Savvy sellers are the experienced consumers who have already bought and sold a home before.

87 percent of savvy sellers have completed at least two home sales in the past.

Their average age is 46 years and

Half of sellers traded up to a larger home in 2006.

Typical home sellers owned their previous home for an average of six years.

Seventy-two percent of savvy sellers are married couples, followed by 17 percent single females.

Savvy sellers need very little education about the selling process, so agents should service these clients with personalized tools like checklists and calendars to help the sellers keep track of key dates—open houses, inspections, and the final closing.

Okay, I've shown you ours; now you need to define yours. Define each of your customer types carefully through segmentation. Position yourself as different and superior, and remember it's about making an experience, not just a sale. What is essential is that you build a true, deep understanding of each of your customers and her needs over time—before, during, and after the transaction. This is key for your entrepreneurial real business to flourish. It starts with asking what she expects and then making a plan to live up to her expectations and exceed them. Just starting out? Customer Relationship Management (CRM) can be as simple as picking up the telephone, sending an e-mail, or initiating an online chat and asking for instant feedback: "Did you like the new product you recently purchased? Did it meet your expectations?" Already have a loyal customer base? Great. Don't forget to ask them how your company can help improve their lives. (It's not just about you and what you're trying to sell. In this layer of the RYI chart, it's all about your customer. Her dreams. Her life and needs.)

> As a customer, I love it when a business is one step ahead of me. The Internet makes this possible. If I give a good retailer a little bit of information, they should be able to impress me.

They can remember birthdays, my preferences, and send me thanks by e-mail. Shutterfly is my new favorite friend. It integrates with my photo software, Picasa, and remembers me when I visit. I recently placed a photo order, and they sent me a thank you note by e-mail. Then they went one step further. They offered me 50 free prints anytime I wanted them. On my next order, I remembered that offer from Shutterfly, but couldn't find the darn e-mail and the code I was sure I needed. After searching my inbox, I gave up trying to find the e-mail thank you. And then, a beautiful thing happened. As I went to check out, the 50 free prints thank you offer was automatically applied! They remembered me, and the promise they'd made.

Neiman Marcus has this down. So does the Ritz. And, well, you have your own list. And yes, these examples are from huge companies that cater to affluent shoppers. But they do know how to make you feel valued, special, and connected to them. You want to buy from them. This kind of treatment goes beyond branding, beyond marketing. It's how you make your customers feel. It's a way to break through to her. Build a bridge, be different, keep changing, and stay interesting. Reward your champions. For example, give her 50 free prints, and she'll sing your praises. It's important to recognize that 20 percent of your customers provide 80 percent of your revenue. Always have, always will.

I'm certain you've had the opposite customer experience, as I have. And you know how it makes you feel. The same day I had the positive online photo experience, I booked travel on a new startup airline at the company's web site. It was late, and I was in a hurry. After I completed the transaction, I realized I'd made an error in the departure date. Reading the confirmation, I was informed there was no customer service, purportedly to save money. There wasn't a phone number either, just an online FAQ list that didn't address my needs. When I sent an e-mail for help, I received an auto-responder telling me to look at the FAQs online. Arrgh. I am lost in customer service nightmare land. So yes, the airline gets points for being there at night, online, when I needed them. But as soon as the sale was over, so was their interest in me. This was a high-ticket transaction—six airline tickets—valued at more than $1,000 and yet nothing but auto-generated e-mails. Not good. Six months and weekly e-mails later, I still haven't received a response . . .

QUESTIONS TO THINK ABOUT

1. What is your plan for customer relationship management? If you aren't familiar with this notion, there are great books on the subject. Don't overthink. Just feel.

2. What is the best example of customer service you've received lately? What specifically did you enjoy about the experience?

3. What is the buying cycle in your business? In real estate, it has averaged seven years. That's a big challenge in retaining customers.

ACTION STEPS

1. Determine the customer buying cycle for your enterprise, and devise a plan of action to respond to it.

2. Create a customer relationship plan, hopefully driven by and supported by technology.

3. What does your best customer feel like if you execute your plan well? Hopefully, she feels the words in layer six of your RYI chart.

A Real Story

Jeni Britton Bauer

Meet Jeni Britton Bauer, born in 1973, president and founder of a specialty food manufacturer, Jeni's Splendid Ice Creams. Business owner since 1996.

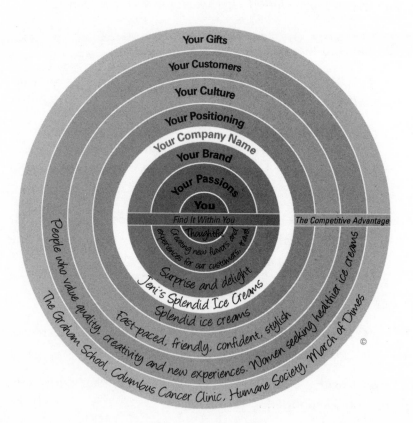

My goal is to provide my customers with surprise and delight. Every day we seek to be surprised ... delightfully. And to bring that experience to our customers through innovative, new products and flavors and four-star service.

Jeni's is stylish, but not faddish—neither in fashion, nor out of fashion. We know our community and love to listen to people and find out what they want. We are friendly and confident. We don't feel like we have to please everyone, but we are absolutely dedicated to making people happy in any way we can.

We find that women love our ice creams because they are a little healthier and because they want to introduce their kids to new and exciting flavors—yes, our flavors can open minds! But really, our target audience is hard to define. We like to say that we make ice cream for our customers, not for everyone. We are proud to be servicing a niche market—we can make people really happy and grow slowly. We tend to know many of our customers personally as well as their tastes, and that's all we care about. We connect with them through our web site, comment cards—and our staff. We closely monitor sales results and listen to our customers, and then plan new flavors based on those sales and customer responses.

The most exciting part of owning your own business is when people appreciate the work that you've done. When you finally get a good review, when customers give great feedback— that's when you feel like all your ideas are finally working!

Jeni learned from the get-go that her customers are savvy. She captures them with a healthier product and fun flavors that taste as good as they sound—lavender and wild berries, coriander with raspberry, and Savannah buttermint. And, she connects with them in all of the right ways so they keep coming back. On her web site—jenisicecreams.com—you can easily order online. You are even invited to visit her test kitchen by calling for an appointment. Hers is a perfect recipe for success.

RECOMMENDED READING

- *Marketing to Women: How to Understand, Reach, and Increase Your Share of the World's Largest Market Segment* by Marti Barletta. An amazing book.

- And for specifics on CRM, read *The CRM Handbook: A Business Guide to Customer Relationship Management* by Jill Dyché.

Life Lesson Eighteen: The real world is online

It's funny I've made this a life lesson. For my kids, this is a duh. They don't know another world. But if you, like me, didn't grow up with a keyboard in your crib, you need a not-so-subtle reminder that this world of paper and books and the like is being replicated, duplicated, and often, made even better online. And I'm not talking about Avatars, Second Life, and Sims stuff. Nope, quite simply, it is vital that your business, no matter what it is or sells, is online. And your online presence must replicate your offline business. You just need to be there. And frankly, as soon as possible, you need to be there with rich media—online videos are the rage, as you know. Present yourself, your real brand, as richly and engagingly as possible. The how is where a great digital marketing consultant can come to your rescue. With the ever-increasing number of digital and mobile options, whatever I would tell you to implement specifically here may be obsolete next year as new options emerge. And it's your real business. You need to know this stuff.

Here is what I do know: Your customers are online, especially your female customers. Women outnumber men online, and it's likely to stay that way.

♦ 2000: Women outnumber men online for the first time, according to Media Matrix.

♦ 2001: Women's online spending has been increasing rapidly, and the gender gap is widening.

♦ 2003: Women made 62 percent of all online purchases, according to BizRate.

♦ 2004: The Internet is the leading media choice for women and trails only work, sleep, and spending time with family across overall activities. It has emerged as the most cherished, most vital medium in women's lives says a study commissioned by Yahoo! and Starcom MediaVest Group.

♦ 2011: Women will comprise 51.9 percent of the total online population and are 51.7 percent today, according to eMarketer.

And even as she is online, she has a lot of things to do there. Research, purchase, learn. Even just 10 years ago, mass media was the message. A broad-based message—placed in the daily newspaper or on the local television station—would reach most of the population of your town and propel your message. Your message could have simply said—hopefully with a smidge of value and creativity—"Buy my widget now," and folks would have responded. Not anymore.

After you've built your online presence, it needs to change and grow. We covered this in the marketing circle in Real Fact 4, but the reason why you need to keep your online presence fresh is that your customer is busy. She is juggling a bunch of roles between family, career, and taking care of herself. At the same time, she is in control of huge amounts of purchasing power— growing daily. There isn't a lot of time to reach her. You can't push messages to her through conventional advertising and expect to get the results past generations could bank on. You've got to engage her online, and keep her there by providing information she can use.

Assign a member of your team—or yourself if you're a sole proprietor—the task of surfing the Web, at least weekly. Take a look at your competitors, type in your keywords—your company's name and yours—and see if anything new is returned on the major search engines. Online social networks spring up daily, on every topic and every product. Where there is an opinion, there's a community for it. And that's where today's consumers hang out. You need to know how you are being talked about online.

Set up a Google alert to notify you when somebody writes about you or your company.

Respond. Return e-mails from your customers immediately if possible. Be there. Busy consumers depend on friends and family for referrals. It's a more powerful endorsement than any expert recommendation—and certainly more influential than any advertising you push on them. And if you don't satisfy them, they'll spread the word. The digital kids—ages 12 and under—will get most of their information from people they know, not from traditional media.

If you haven't been to wikipedia.org, go there. Create an entry page in Wikipedia for your Real brand. Make a list of every page on Wikipedia that relates to your brand, and check them often, or set up a feed. Don't cite what is posted there in a paper for school—just ask my sophomore—but your Real You Incorporated brand needs to be there. The real world is there.

Social networks can also be organized around business connections, as in the case of linkedin.com. If you haven't created a free account, do that now, too. You can search by school names, company names, web sites, and more to find people—people you may have even forgotten about—who are also online.

We've mentioned facebook.com and its growing business applications as another place where you should be. Reconnect. Network. Keep building your Real brand through your online community. The newest social networks on the Internet are focused on niches such as travel, art, sports, cars, dog owners, investors, and even cosmetic surgery. Other social networking sites focus on local communities, sharing local business and entertainment reviews, news, event calendars, and happenings. Even megasite amazon.com has created a social network, askville.com.

At Real Living, we created MyRealLiving 2.0 just for these customers. While we'd had a consumer-facing web site since 2002, and broker-owner and agent intranet business center since the late 1990s, we hadn't created a consumer-focused portal. Launched in 2005, MyRealLiving 2.0 puts our consumers in control, which was a big change for the real estate industry. Once in her password-protected site, our customer can select her agent or multiple agents, begin dialogue with them, accept appointments, save searches, and share communications with her friends and family. All communication is directed by the consumer, not us. The next generation of MyRealLiving will offer even more features—more opportunity for user-generated content and more social networking. We're asking our customers what they want, Individually, and they tell us. More power, more information, more help sorting and selecting online. Once our buyers find their new homes, the MyRealLiving portal converts into their My Home page, where the customer can save all documents related to the process and more. This is, I think, where the future is online. Private spaces where a customer can learn about your Real brand and engage with you when she'd like to do so. Think about what this means to your business.

See the following page for the Real Living web site at this moment in time. (Although it better look different if you visit today.) We refresh the imagery and messaging often while keeping

the heart of our brand in place. Notice the invitation to join MyRealLiving is prominent.

Now it's not one size or product or service fits all. Widget choice is everywhere, and what you and your Real You business must do is focus on your specific customers as tightly as possible. It's niche marketing, the notion of defining as much as possible your specific target audience and providing a product or service to match her needs. By the way, *niche* is derived from the Latin word for *nest*. Are you making your customers feel safe and valued? This would be the opposite of inviting everybody to buy your widget. A niche marketer in the new economy would create a pink mini-widget that fits snugly in her purse. The pink widget would be advertised online, everywhere pink widget purchasers are. With

technology, you can target messages and become interactive with your customers. With smaller, customized businesses and new distribution options by way of e-commerce, the world is your oyster. Not broadly, but specifically. It's about customizing your product or service to the specific interests of your customer niches. The future of marketing is niche marketing, and your success depends on this. Loyalty from your customers demands it. The more you know about her and her needs, the more predictable revenue you reap, the better lifetime value you enjoy, and the more positive word of mouth you will receive.

So, as you're focusing in on the needs and experiences you'll provide to your target niche audience, your Real You

Incorporated brand will be behind you. That's because you are your business. You're authentic, and your customers will feel it. Anticipate her needs. Invite her comments and ideas. Forget about the old days of passive push marketing, and harness digital marketing, events, and environmental branding to pull your customers to you. Your Real You Incorporated brand has a voice and a purpose: To make your customer feel something. Experience something. To connect with you. Stay real, keep a fresh web presence, and your venture will thrive.

QUESTIONS TO THINK ABOUT

1. Can you envision five of your best customers? If you haven't launched yet, imagine who they will be.

2. What could you do to delight these customers online? At Real Living, we've created a series of quizzes for customers to discover their decorating style, housing types, and more.

3. What other products and services do your best niche customers spend time and money on? Would you consider enticing them with a password-protected site just for them?

ACTION STEPS

1. Imagine a day in her life. At Real Living, we've defined seven niche consumer types we want to get to know. These are mega-niches, big groups of women. Our goal is to grow ever closer to these consumers with every interaction. Start to paint a picture of these niches or niche, and describe how your product or service will make her life easier.

2. The digital landscape changes daily. Subscribe to blogs and e-newsletters within your industry, and keep current.

3. Go where your customers are online. Find out what they read and where they spend time. You and your brand are just a small part of her life. Always remember that.

A Real Story

Kim Ades

Meet Kim Ades, born in 1968, owner of Opening Doors and Frame of Mind Coaching, specializing in thought management, and contributing sales and marketing writer. Business owner since 1990.

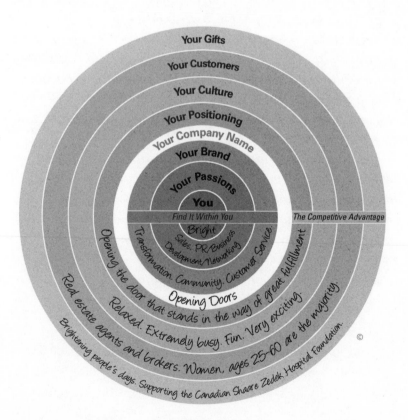

I am an entrepreneur through and through—it's in my blood, my nature, my character. Owning multiple businesses, from a balloon decorating company to a coaching services firm, I realized early on that having an online presence is absolutely critical to success in today's business world. At a very basic level, it is the indicator that you actually exist as a business, and it gives you some degree of credibility in the market. At a more advanced level, it is a strategic way to extend your exposure to your target market, increase your revenues, and even increase the overall value of your business. The more extensive your reach, the greater your success.

The majority of my customers are women, ages 25 to 60. Where are they? Online, of course. But launching a static Web site isn't going to persuade people to visit often. It's important to keep people interested and captivated—this is one of the keys involved in developing a loyal customer base. For this reason, keeping your online presence as up to date as possible is vital. It tells a story, it keeps people coming back for more, and it shows that as a business owner, you are on top of your game. One way to keep your content fresh is through blogging.

I love blogging and get tons of positive feedback on my blog. At the end of the day, people do business with people they like and trust. I find that the blogging platform allows you to expose the personal side of who you are and gives clients the opportunity to buy into you as a human being. For me, it's a mode of expression and a place to develop a library of relevant collateral materials that tell a series of compelling stories of who I am, my philosophy, my experiences, and my frame of mind.

Kim knows her customer and knows how to reach her—online. She's embracing new technologies and expressing her Real self through them. Experimenting is good. But blogging isn't for everyone. You have to love to write and be devoted to posting almost daily. You don't want to let down your followers and customers.

RECOMMENDED READING

♦ Jump online. Shop online. Research online. Get carried away by the power of social networking. Set up a Facebook profile for your business. Join LinkedIn. Read about other businesses in your industry. Use the power of the Web to grow yourself, and your business. Do it today.

In this Real Fact, you've discovered your customers and how to keep your arms around them. You've learned:

♦ Customers know if you're faking it

♦ Be everywhere she wants you to be

♦ The real world is online

Your RYI chart is almost complete.

Women entrepreneurs tend to fight for their own identity. And in the process, become strong.

Lois Wyse

your gifts

REAL FACT #7
Chart Uncharted Waters

Here we are. The last Real Fact for your RYI chart. In this circle, you will define what your gifts are to the world. You know yourself, your passions, your brand essence. You know what your brand looks like in the world and the niche—large or small—that defines your customers. And you know what experience they will encounter with your real brand. Finally, we need to document the gifts you'll bring to the world both through your business and outside your business. These are, of course, the people and community treasures you invest in with your time and your money. This is your legacy we're talking about here, and for women it has always been about more than leaving a successful business, although that can certainly be a part.

Hopefully you had a mentor, a positive role model for your dreams. You didn't get here alone, even if it feels lonely along the way. Many of our Real Story profilees in this book couldn't name a mentor, but acknowledged the influence other women have had from afar. You should, too. Some of those women might include: Estee Lauder, Jenny Craig, Helena Rubenstein, Anne Klein, Margaret Rudkin (she founded Pepperidge Farms in the 1930s), Ruth Fertel (Ruth's Chris Steak House), Mary Ellen Sheets (Two Men and A Truck), Sheryl Leach (Barney in 1988), Lillian Vernon Katz, Anita Roddick (The Body Shop), Lane Bryant, Diane von Furstenberg, Mary Kay Ash, Lane Nemuth (Discovery Toys), Lois Wyse (Wyse Advertising), Kate Spade, and so on and so on. So, even if you don't have one, pick a famous trailblazer to be yours. Learn her story. Share it and then become the woman another woman is proud to call her mentor.

When you find inspiration outside yourself, and spread the story of that inspiration, you are giving a gift to the world. For empowering women inspiration, my favorite magazine is *Pink*. For marketing it's *Advertising Age,* with an occasional trade publication such as *LORE* or RIS Media's *Real Estate* magazine thrown in for good measure. But back to *Pink*. *Pink* was founded by women for women. I first picked up a copy at a Delta's Crown Room, where it was distributed for free. I think I was one of the founding subscribers, as I read that issue from cover to cover. The thing about *Pink* is that every page holds an inspiration, someone you probably don't know but who will share a nugget about herself that makes you more confident with yourself. Make sense?

It's lonely enough at the top. When you take yourself as seriously as we do when we're being real, you need to engage in work you value, and you need to share those beliefs. Not just at the office. But throughout your community, however wide and deep your community becomes. It may never be Oprah-sized, but your impact can be just as deep. Happy, Real women nurture the next generation. It sounds like a cliché, but giving back always brings you more.

And finally, happy Real women nurture the next generation of women, salute the ones who came before us, and keep busting through barriers at every step along the way. And that truly makes for a well-rounded, real woman entrepreneur.

So welcome to the final layer of the RYI chart: your gifts. They are plentiful. This Real Fact's aim is to help you identify the ones you'd like to share with the world. In the end, there is no true success without significance, without leaving a positive legacy. In this Real Fact, these life lessons will be covered:

- ◆ Build your business network

- ◆ Change the world for other women

- ◆ Capture your charitable passion

As Diane von Furstenberg said, "I take risks. I dive in. I'm passionate—yet it's an act of passion that makes things happen." I'd add, it's also an act of *compassion* that makes things happen.

Life Lesson Nineteen: Build your business network

You are an entrepreneur because you're seeking flexibility, control of your work life, and freedom to do things your way. But what you can't forget is the fourth leg of the stool: connections.

Compared with men, women are more likely to have networks that include family and friends, or networks with higher proportions of family members. That can be good and bad. Women with family members as their primary network don't have access to meaningful information or new leads compared to women who have professional, business networks. This lack of networking outside the family can hurt you the most during the startup phase of your Real You Incorporated business. Let's face it, your mom may not be the best source for financing advice, suggesting lawyers or accountants, or referring business books. We are the caretakers in our society and carry the bulk of the family obligations. Still. But while family is great in helping to run a business and provide support, they can't be your only sounding board. Think diversity.

Who you know is essential in business and developing your competitive advantage network. Connections are key, and business associates can help provide you with the confidence you need to get going and stay motivated. I know I get torn between attending my WPO meetings and making a soccer game for my sixth-grader. Usually, the soccer game wins. But really, half of the time it should be soccer, the other half building my network.

It's critical to network with different people—people who don't work for you and aren't related to you—to get different perspectives.

> Diversity of opinions and backgrounds, that's what keeps you real, keeps your perspective fresh.

If everybody you talk to has a similar background and experience level, you won't receive true advice or feedback. And you, as a real entrepreneur, want to surround yourself with people who can teach you something new, challenge your assumptions, and propel you to greatness.

Let's assume you don't know everyone you need to know to grow your business. Who does? That's when the networking game comes into play. Even if you're an introvert, as an entrepreneurial businesswoman, you've got to reach out. And it's not just a numbers game. You're a real person, building business relationships on trust and respect. So how do you do that? Keep the basics of business networking at heart.

Tip 1

You need to be able to ask for business. If that's hard for you, practice. Seriously. It's called the elevator pitch for good reason. You need to be able to articulate, in a quick sentence or two, your keywords: name, company's name, your business or industry, your product, and where to find you. Followed closely by, "and here's my business card." All in the span of an elevator going up a couple of floors. Remember that adage, you only have one chance to make a good first impression. At the writer's conferences I've been to recently, as much of the focus is on perfecting your pitch as it is on perfecting your writing. It's the same for any industry.

Tip 2

And speaking of business cards, never leave home without them. Evenings. Weekends. Always. Successful real estate agents know this, and you should, too. Cards are cheap, be generous with them. (Of course, they have your e-mail address, phone, and web site listed.) Hand them to friends and family, and give them your elevator pitch. Explain to them your target audience. Practice with them, and they'll be able to share your vision. Ask for referrals, maximize every chance meeting and swap cards.

Tip 3

Once your pitch is perfected, your cards are printed, and your friends and family are onboard, you need to make sure you're memorable. Be distinctive and take a genuine interest in people. Remember, everyone can spot a fake. Start with small talk and work your way up to meaningful talk. Pay attention. Reach out to someone else standing alone. And, with 420 women in the United States starting their own business each day, you need to stand out in the crowd. It's no longer going to be true that being a woman business owner makes you unique. Now it's about the real you.

Tip 4

Join organizations that have meaning to you. Do you want to go to meetings to learn or to just make contacts? Visit as many groups as possible before joining any because you need to be selective. Attending too many meetings or joining too many groups is the opposite of real. And when you decide which organization is for you, become an active member. Take on a leadership role. You'll get the most out of your time and membership that way, and so will the organization.

Tip 5

Use the Internet for networking. Beyond posting your profile and your business's profile on the popular social networking sites, know there are a number of small business networking sites out there as well. Many focus on women entrepreneurs, others on specific types of businesses. Some of these networking sites have fees attached; and some offer free memberships, including: eacademy.com, thewildwe.com, mominventors.com, ladieswholaunch.com, homeofficewomen.com, women-wave.org braveheartwomen.org, sisterkeeper.org, and everywoman.co.uk in England. Visit realyouincorporated.com for more.

Tip 6

As a woman-owned business, you need to consider applying for certification with the Women's Business Enterprise National Council at wbenc.org. Another rich site, full of free information, is womenowned.com. Check out womenentrepreneur.com for great networking ideas.

Tip 7

During face-to-face or online networking, remember to give as well as to take. Ask open-ended questions of others, and truly listen. You need to actively build relationships, not databases of business cards and e-mail addresses. Speaking of that, though, do stay organized. And e-mail is fine once you've started a relationship. In fact, according to the Meta Group Survey, 80 percent of people prefer typing to talking. Think about what that means for your networking strategies.

Tip 8

Don't underestimate the power of women's organizations. You need to realize that without them, you wouldn't be creating your real business today. I'm serious. It takes groups of women joining together to affect change. As you grow your Real You Incorporated business, engaging in the work you love and building a culture you're proud of, you need to realize that almost no woman has had an unimpeded career. I hope the next generation will be able to say they have, but until now, we haven't. We need to talk, as Joan Rivers would say. I am a member of the WPO, the Women Presidents' Organization. It's empowering and great for business. I'm new to my group, so while they've been together for a while, I'm just getting to know them. They are a diverse and powerful collection of women of all ages, backgrounds, and businesses. Once you start searching around online, you'll be amazed by all the women's networking opportunities. Another great organization is the National Association of Women Business Owners, nawbo.org, created to strengthen the wealth-creating capacity of women business owners.

In your quest to keep learning and adding to your network, don't be afraid to reach out to other business people you admire, no matter how famous or seemingly out of reach. They are people, too, and if you make the interchange mutually beneficial, you'll be surprised at the results. I write a weekly column for a local newspaper chain called, aptly, "Connections." It is about people and events, important and not so important. But truly, it's about relationships in the central Ohio community. The point of this story, beyond the obvious point that connections are of vital importance to your business, is that I never would have agreed to write it without my editor, Ben Cason. The newspaper chain had been wooing me to write a column for years, but until Ben came to town from the *Washington Post*, I had turned them down.

I knew I could learn a lot from Ben. I still do—about writing, about the newspaper business, about politics, about people. We have great, two-hour lunches whenever possible. As a mentor and a boss, he's my longest-standing survivor. His insights into my real estate business are invaluable, too, and come from an entirely different perspective from anyone else's in my network.

Find people who can teach you something new. Collect them. Nurture them. They are an important part of your competitive advantage.

QUESTIONS TO THINK ABOUT

1. Who are your top five business advisers? Are too many of them related to you? Employed by you? This would be an ideal group: one family member, one friend, one co-worker, one business entrepreneur in another category, one consultant, and one fellow group or association member. How does your close network stack up?

2. Conversely, don't confuse your business network with your personal network, otherwise you'll turn socializing into networking, and that's not real. Don't confuse a to-do list with your relaxing, fun list. Even as a business owner, you need time just to be. Remember your friend list from Real Fact 2? Don't go it alone. Those are the You people. They are a different group from your competitive advantage network. There can be overlap, but not much. Do you understand the difference?

3. Variety is the spice of life. Make sure your personal and competitive advantage networks are enriched with different types of people.

ACTION STEPS

1. Make a list of your top business advisers.

2. Make a list of business and industry organizations you feel would be worthwhile to become involved with. Research them. Join at least two. Join a women's entrepreneurial or business group—WPO, WBENC, or another of your choice. Women only. Do that today. Visit Forte Foundation's (fortefoundation.org) entrepreneur tab for a great list of women's entrepreneurial organizations.

3. Purchase a subscription to *Pink* magazine. Other choices include: *Savvy Women's Magazine, Working Woman, Enterprising Women*, and *Working Mother*. Just as I hope you've found inspiration reading this book, you will get a monthly or bimonthly dose of inspiration from each of these publications. Cool, free inspiration delivered to your inbox can be found by signing up for a free e-newsletter from womenandbiz.com. The UK's *Real Business* magazine—for women—has a great web site of inspiration, too: realbusiness.co.uk/women.

A Real Story

Marsha Firestone, Ph.D.

Meet Marsha Firestone, born in 1943, president and
founder, Women Presidents' Organization. Business
owner since 1997.

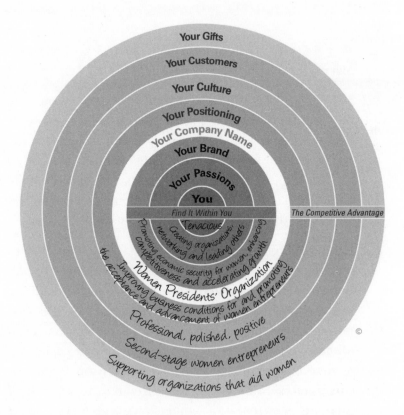

When women entrepreneurs reach a certain level, I call them second-stage entrepreneurs—they learn the most from their peers. It is well documented and researched. Peer knowledge is invaluable. Peers share their experiences and expertise. That's what the WPO meetings are for—that's how women at this level should learn.

My peers, who include Susan Bari, Meryl Unger, and Adrienne Hall, and I share many ideas with one another. I've learned a lot from the entrepreneurs in the WPO. Each brings something to the discussion.

The idea for launching WPO came to me when I was working for the American Woman's Economic Development Corporation, a nonprofit that helped startup and young women entrepreneurs. I realized they needed a program specifically for those women business owners who had already achieved success. So, when they were considering me to become president of the organization, I made a proposal to create the WPO. When they didn't choose me for president, it gave me the impetus to leave. I was sad and disappointed about not being selected, but it ended up being the best professional decision that could have happened. It set me free to go out and get more experience. For me, this was a great life lesson. Of course, I think fate had a lot to do with it, too.

At WPO, our mission is to improve business conditions for women entrepreneurs and to promote the acceptance and advancement of women entrepreneurs in all industries.

We are a growing worldwide community of entrepreneurs participating in a forum that leverages resources to fulfill aspirations, achieve economic equality, and promote well-being. The organization provides continuing education and peer mentoring in business and leadership to women entrepreneurs and serves as a resource for developing solutions to the unique problems and challenges encountered by women entrepreneurs. The Women Presidents' Organization is the ultimate destination for women in business.

Marsha knows it can be lonely at the top, so she created an organization for female entrepreneurs to help them build their business network. You could join a similar group, or follow Marsha's lead and create something less formal in your community. The important point is to branch out.

RECOMMENDED READING

♦ *How to Work a Room, Revised Edition: Your Essential Guide to Savvy Socializing* by Susan RoAne. An authority and the original expert on working a room, she provides great tips to even the most reluctant networkers. Read it before your next networking event.

Life Lesson Twenty: Change the world for other women

The first wave of feminism opened the crack for female corporate ladder climbers and entrepreneurs. These women worked so hard to achieve their dreams that many didn't have the time or energy to mentor women following in their footsteps. The competition to get to and stay at the top consumed them. I recently spoke to one such woman who, now in her mid 70s and still working, is a shining example of surviving in a male-dominated business world. We celebrate her as a true pioneer, and she is. But her method of getting to the top, and staying there all these years, feels somehow unreal to those of us in the latter waves. During our discussion, I asked her what she was doing to help the mostly 30-something-year-old women in her department develop their skills. How is she mentoring the next generation and the next?

"I put her name in for a committee," she answered. "I'm going out of my way to help her." No, not really. That sort of gesture, recommending or nominating your protégés for positions within trade associations and the like, is expected. So is spending time answering questions, hiring women whenever possible, making sure they are paid equally, and pointing out discrimination whenever you see it is all expected.

We need to really help one another, especially as we redefine business and entrepreneurship in the twenty-first century. Together, we have the economic and social power to change the world. But divided, we don't. That means spanning the generations and appreciating the women who paved the way. Like Susan B. Anthony. Like Gloria Steinem. Like your first female boss, whether she was an entrepreneur or not. Because here's the thing: Women still make almost 30 cents less per hour than men for the same job. That's way better than the 52 cents made by women to a man's dollar in the 1970s, but it's not good enough. Violence against women is still couched in terms like "domestic disturbance." It's offensive to say, "the girls in the office," but that phrase persists. There are still not enough women on corporate boards. We have or will have daughters, and your friends will have daughters and so on. Every one of us needs to be a social change agent for women and girls. It takes one to know one. And, no, you don't need to burn a bra to make a start.

So, how can you help support other women? One of my favorite methods is through support of The Women's Fund movement. Quite simply, Women's Funds across the country raise money from women to invest back into the community to support women and girls. It's women in action with a purpose, and you should consider joining one in your city or start one yourself. It's about building a community of women who use their money to invest in other women to change lives. Another opportunity to empower women is through the YWCA. I support the local Women's Fund in my community and the YWCA. I am on the board of the latter. I know, you may be thinking that you already operate a business, manage employees and clients, and run a household. I know there are only so many hours in a day. If you don't have extra time, right now, there are organizations that need your resources as well. Then, find a way to work in the time angle, too. It's that simple. Period. Can you imagine what all our lives would be like without women who stood up for other women?

Tell the stories of the women who are famous for the first two waves, and share your own stories.

> And along the way, make sure you acknowledge, as much as possible, that the choices your mom made, the choices the generation before you made, were all made in relation to the times they lived in.

Context is key. You will never experience the same climate the generation before you experienced as equal rights keep getting pushed forward by some famous women, but mostly by those who are not. It really takes all of us speaking, writing, and talking.

The Internet makes it possible. You'll find an abundance of information on how to change the world with just a click. The Internet has provided women with the space to give voice to their needs, and share injustices and victories. More sustainable than the activist feminist groups of the 1960s and 1970s, today's feminist movement is composed of hundreds of web sites, thousands of blogs, and millions of e-mails. The power of technology allows more women entrepreneurs to work from home, if they choose, and stay connected and successful, while daily it becomes ever-more affordable to the lower-income members of society who are, not surprisingly, more often women and children. It's the great equalizer in so many ways.

You have the power to get inspired. Make some new connections. Reach up and down through the generations. Web sites and organizations with great information include: Catalyst (catalyst.org), the leading nonprofit corporate membership research and advisory organization working globally with businesses and professionals to build inclusive environments and expand opportunities for women and business, and the Forte Foundation (fortefoundation.org), a growing community of women, ready to share ideas about the workplace, professional development, and work-life balance. More traditionally feminist sites to visit include feminist.com and the National Organization for Women (NOW) (now.org), the organization that picked up where the suffragettes left off.

As women, we define our success in the world not just by profits made, but also by our role and impact in the greater community. Given that fact, the more women you help achieve their dreams, the better the world becomes for all. It's a circular notion. Hopefully, after reading this life lesson, you've added empowering women to your list of gifts in the final circle of your RYI chart.

QUESTIONS TO THINK ABOUT

1. Do you feel uncomfortable calling yourself a feminist? Probably. Most people do. So turn the noun into an action verb and talk about empowering women. Does that feel okay?

2. How have you helped another woman this week, either at work or at home or both?

3. Have you thought about how you can nurture the next generation of women?

ACTION STEPS

1. Empower another woman today with a kind word, a reference, or taking a mentee to lunch.

2. Have you asked another woman how you can help her achieve her dreams lately? Ask.

3. Give your money. Time alone will not change the world, and vice versa. Get involved. Get committed. Use the power of your purse, your brain, and your imagination. You are an unstoppable, real entrepreneur.

A Real Story

Kelley McBride Quinn

Meet Kelley McBride Quinn, born in 1960, pilates
and yoga therapist and owner of The Bodywell, LLC.
Business owner since 1999.

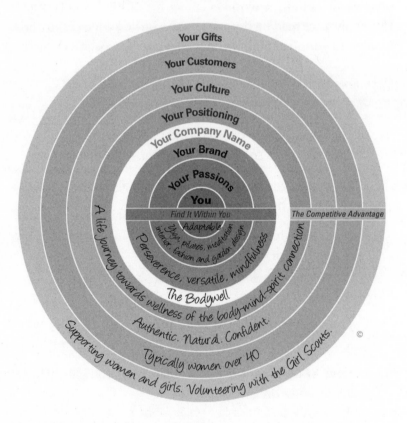

I am the mother of two daughters, ages 6 and 10, so, not surprisingly, I'm focusing my energies on young women. I volunteer my time as a Girl Scout leader. I am also in the beginning stages of creating a program for teenage girls in my community that empowers them to identify, maintain, and grow their authentic voices through art and movement therapies.

I developed the program for girls ages 9 to 14 to complete my studies in a two-year advanced yoga training program. The goal is to help girls with the issue of female relational aggression, more commonly known as "girl bullying." I believe that practicing yoga during early adolescence may actually alter the course of their lives, helping young girls to realize their full potential while supplying them with the resources to foster healthy relationships. The program is meant to address the issues shared by the victim, her aggressor, and those caught in the middle.

Over the years, I have had great teachers who have inspired me to be myself and to share the gifts I have to offer with others. My heartfelt hope for my daughters and all young women is that they stay true to themselves—to the God-given gifts that are uniquely their own. And to never feel that they must be silenced if their desired path is one that society says is not acceptable for a woman.

If more of us followed Kelley's lead, what a better place it would be, not just for young girls and women, but for everyone. Kelley has found a meaningful way to give back that involves her passion and her personal life. Be inspired by her example. You can do the same. Do your research, think about it, and then find a way to empower women today. The sooner you start, the better you'll feel.

RECOMMENDED READING

♦ *Queen Bees and Wannabes: Helping Your Daughter Survive Cliques, Gossip, Boyfriends, and Other Realities of Adolescence,* by Rosalind Wiseman, is a fantastic book and will remind, quite painfully, of what it was like for you growing up. Slang has changed, but not much else. Middle school and high school were where you learned much of your survival—ah—socialization skills. Read it for you, and then read it to help your daughter or a friend's daughter.

♦ If you have a daughter and she's not at the "mean girl" stage, read *The Paper Bag Princess* by Robert N. Munsch with her, and she'll know she can always slay her own dragons.

Life Lesson Twenty-One: Capture your charitable passion

Throughout *Real You Incorporated,* we've made a point of staying true to the real you within all of your business adventures, and that also means that your business cannot become your only passion. Don't get so caught up in your to-do list that you forget your to-be list. It's lonely being an entrepreneur without isolating yourself. As we covered in Life Lesson Nineteen, entrepreneurial success comes from building a network, a support system of people who boost your confidence and propel your dreams.

Another key ingredient is community involvement. It just is. It's in our DNA as women to care about more than ourselves. Connecting and reaching out to others is natural for us. Sustainable, real enterprises leave a legacy of caring for not only their families and their businesses, but also for their community. Real brands have a philanthropic bent that is felt throughout the entire organization.

As always, this starts with you. Women business owners are philanthropically active. According to the Center for Women's Business Research, 68 percent volunteer at least once a month, 31 percent contribute $5,000 or more annually to charities, and 15 percent give $10,000 or more. Capturing your charitable passion and sharing it with your employees begins to change not only your company, enriching it immeasurably, but also helps change the world for the better. The full potential of female business owners to make the world a better, much more real and caring place is so palpable and will be part of the third wave of feminism. And that will be an amazing legacy to be a part of, don't you think?

> So, if you're not fully engaged in a charitable pursuit, how do you get there? You follow your heart. Pay attention to the needs in your community, and when it feels right, respond.

You don't need to have a personal experience with the problem, though many women find the passion to give back comes from there. They were helped by the YWCA as a girl, so they donate time and money there now. Or, they escaped an abusive relationship and now donate time and money to the battered women's shelter. If your passion isn't from a past life experience, though, that doesn't devalue it once you discover it.

Back in the late 1980s, when I was working at that first advertising agency, for that miserable boss, I saw a story on the local television news about homeless families. Until that time,

I hadn't given homelessness more than a passing thought. I was captivated by the sadness of the fact there was no homeless shelter for families in our town. Moms and girls went to the women's shelter; men and boys over 12 to the men's shelter. The last thing these families had was each other, and they were being broken apart. Horrible. Well, I became obsessed with helping them, and the result—Make Room Columbus—was the first shelter for homeless families in my community. It was an all-volunteer effort. Leading a group of 200-plus volunteers on a mission not only helped those homeless families, but helped me grow personally, too. I met fabulous, committed social service workers and shelter operators. I met committed professionals from across all business types in Columbus and boosted my business network. Most important, it makes me to this day an informed advocate for homeless families and kids. My passion led me there. I never was homeless—although people who didn't know me often asked that at the time. I just knew the situation was wrong. And if I believed we could fix it, I knew others would, too. And they did.

The point: Follow your charitable passion. What needs in the community match with your gifts? Or is there a national or international issue that tugs at your heart? Are you moved by the plight of homeless animals? Affordable day care or elder care? The environment? Inner-city school kids? The arts? Religious outreach? A medical issue, like asthma or diabetes? A mental health issue, like ADD or depression? An environmental issue, like global warming? An international crisis, like the AIDS epidemic? What about empowering women or eliminating racism? Both are goals of the YWCA, the oldest women's social organization, by the way.

At Real Living, we launched the Real Living Green initiative in response to a heartfelt belief among our franchisees and agents that we could help spread the word about green living at home.

Through education and engaging tools on our web site, we hope to make our customers aware of their households' carbon footprints and how to reduce them. Being the first major player in the real estate industry to promote eco-friendly practices, we know we well help encourage others to follow.

If you're passionate about helping, there is a charity or a cause that needs you. And, if no one is addressing your passion, well, there's another entrepreneurial opportunity for you. And while you are giving your time and money—it really should be a combination of both—you will be receiving in turn. According to the Center for Women's Business Research, 92 percent of all women make financial contributions to charity. Add your heart and your passion, and that financial contribution will turn to gold. The combination of compassion, fueled by passion, is unstoppable.

QUESTIONS TO THINK ABOUT

1. What problems in your community or the world are the most important to you?

2. Is there a natural fit between your Real You Incorporated business and a community need?

3. Passion with a purpose drives your business life. Imagine if your charitable life overlapped with your business life. It could be an unstoppable combination.

ACTION STEPS

1. Pick three areas where your gifts could shine and probably have in the past. Write down three areas of your charitable philanthropic passion. Those will form the outer layer of your RYI chart.

2. Seek out organizations in your community that serve at least one of your chosen areas. If an organization addresses more than one, even better. Write these down. Check out the helpful web site volunteermatch.org for ideas.

3. Decide how and if your business will become involved in your charitable passion. Create a personal and business philanthropy plan. To get started, visit futureofphilanthropy.org where you'll find ideas, checklists, and sample plans.

A Real Story

Barbara Fergus

Meet Barbara Fergus, born in 1935, owner and partner of an automotive dealership, Midwestern Auto Group (MAG), and community activist and philanthropist. In business since 1992.

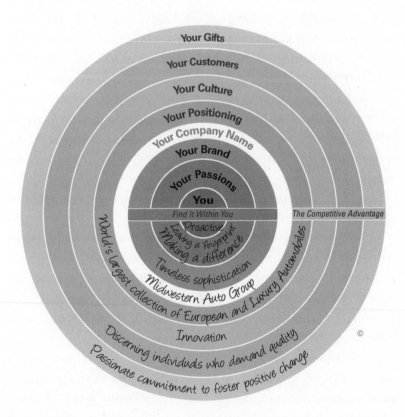

I believe that whoever you are and whatever you do, you need to make a contribution. It is an old-fashioned word, but we are "obliged" to share our knowledge and our talents. It is not enough to lead by example. You must encourage and nurture others to join in. One person with passion, innovation, and dedication is a powerful force, 10 people are a force that demands attention, and 100 people are a force unto themselves that demands results. A collaborative investment is spiritually, emotionally, and intellectually liberating, allowing the group to be risk-takers, entrepreneurs, and courageous visionaries who can accomplish great things beyond the normal expectations of an individual. It is, after all, not our singular achievements that define us, but rather our shared experiences that uplift us.

My philanthropy is multifaceted. I believe when possible, if you see a need, you fill a need. And yet, I have a special interest in arts and culture. They represent the soul of a city. Historically, it has often been the arts that define a civilization by transcending all obstacles. Arts and culture communicate in a universal language that creates a commonality in our increasingly global village. The importance of a thriving arts community cannot be overstated.

Of equal interest is strengthening women's leadership. All recent studies show that how we treat and care for our women and children is a clear reflection on the overall health and well-being of society. With that in mind, the fact that women, who are the leading-edge academics, activists, executives, entrepreneurs, and practitioners are still making only 70 cents for every dollar earned by a man is a sad commentary. We must welcome everyone to the table to participate equally in a thoughtful, challenging, and occasionally rebellious dialogue. It is only through public policy and policy change that long-lasting positive results can be achieved. We need to embrace change. For the simple truth is, if you want to change the world, you have to allow the world to change you.

Barbara's philanthropy is an example of passion with a purpose. She examines what's important to her, and then proceeds with focus to make real change. It doesn't stop there, though. She encourages others to follow her lead. That's an unstoppable domino effect.

RECOMMENDED READING

♦ *Inspired Philanthropy: Your Step-by-Step Guide to Creating a Giving Plan* (Second Edition), by Tracy Gary and Melissa Kohner, teaches you how to create a giving plan and align it with your passions and values.

♦ For a broader perspective on philanthropy, *The Greater Good: How Philanthropy Drives the American Economy and Can Save Capitalism,* by Claire Gaudiani, is a passionate and optimistic book with solutions for continuing philanthropic gift-giving in the United States.

Hats off to you. Now you have a completed your RYI chart. So far, you've learned:

♦ Your future starts now

♦ Learn from your past

♦ Describe yourself in a word

♦ Find the real people in your life

♦ Don't go it alone

- Follow your instincts

- Tell your company story

- Define your brand essence

- Create your vision statement

- The five senses of branding

- Create a marketing plan

- Make it tangible, even if it's virtual

- Be a creative leader

- Express your brand in hiring

- Avoid culture vultures

- Customers know if you're faking it

- Be everywhere she wants you to be

- The real world is online

- Build your business network

- Capture your charitable passion

- Change the world for other women

Take a moment to applaud your accomplishment. Personal and business introspection aren't easy tasks. But now that your journey is complete, you have a guide for the rest of your life. Congratulations! In the final Real Fact, we celebrate you and your business with some words of inspiration and three final life lessons.

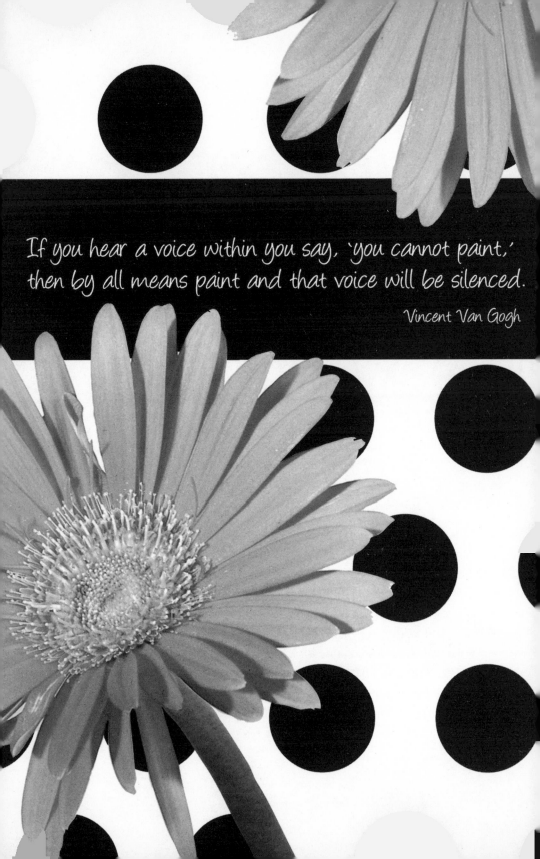

If you hear a voice within you say, 'you cannot paint,' then by all means paint and that voice will be silenced.

Vincent Van Gogh

Creativity Is Unstoppable
(And yes, we're talking business here)

Originally, my editor wanted this this Real Fact to be titled *Businesses that Work for Women,* or something like that. Well, you know my answer to that. All businesses work for women. You can do anything you set your mind on as long as it ties to your Real You and your true passions. Be true to yourself, and you're on your way. Thinking of a new, better way to do or make something certainly fits, as does the ability to feed a baby while simultaneously interviewing an important source for a story. I have to note that of the women entrepreneurs I've met and read about, I am in awe of the moms out there who truly do it all.

This Real Fact is a gift to you, our thanks to you for becoming a Real You Incorporated entrepreneur. Go forth and prosper as we leave you with these final life lessons that all swirl around the notion of creativity, positive momentum, and believing in yourself. Don't forget to visit us online at www.realyouincorporated.com. No homework here, just some encouragement and, hopefully, a little inspiration, too:

♦ Don't get stuck

♦ Play

♦ Share

Life Lesson Twenty-Two: Don't get stuck

It's so hard to see it when you're in the middle of it. We're in the middle of a huge cultural shift and a groundswell of empowered women. You're also in the middle of self-fulfillment through your entrepreneurial dreams. But just as your dreams for your business come true, you still are in the middle of all of your other commitments … your life, your family's life, your—well—whatever. The key here is: Don't get stuck and quit. Times are changing faster than they ever have. Technology is bounding forward, and yet, you and I are here. In the middle of it. Building lives. Building businesses.

I was shopping recently at one of my favorite places, and the owner, a single-store success story, shared with me how she'd like to find investors for expansion. The problem is, she related, women entrepreneurs' access to capital is lagging far behind our industriousness. This will change as banks recognize that the number of wealthy women around the globe continues to grow at twice the rate of men. And, that it's just good business to invest in them.

For the past two decades, the majority of women-owned firms have continued to grow at around two times the rate of all firms, according to the Center for Women's Business Research.

The recognition of our collective power has a long way to go. According to a Kauffman Foundation report, women possess more than half the nation's wealth but account for less than 8 percent of the angel (startup) investment community. As my retailer friend would tell you, it's hard to know where to turn. My advice: Start asking. This will keep you from getting stuck. Begin sharing your vision and your dream with your network, and tap into their networks. Go online. Go to events. There are women entrepreneur events springing up daily, all over. Check them out, and make sure they're a good fit. And if you're looking for financing, be sure you attend investment-oriented conferences targeted to entrepreneurs.

Because if you don't ask, you certainly won't find funding. Women traditionally have been socialized against self-promotion, so you have to overcome that tendency. Start networking. Many women feel they don't want outside control in their business. If that's you, that's okay. Control may be the reason you started in the first place. But if lack of funding is getting you stuck, change your tactic. And remember, think big and go for it! We're all changing the world one bank, one venture capitalist, and one angel funder at a time.

When I get stuck, I think of women to inspire me. I would be remiss if I didn't share my personal thanks to Gloria Steinem. Without her, many of us wouldn't be writing books about women entrepreneurs or going for it. Even now, in her 70s, she takes the stage and inspires. She recently came to a Women's Fund event in Columbus, Ohio. I couldn't believe she was coming, and I couldn't wait to go. (The fact that my fourth-grader's final orchestra performance eventually landed on the same date, same time, is another story. Ah, working momdom.) Anyway, I started to ask the talented young women who work for me if they would like to go see her. Who? She sounds familiar," they would say Harumph. I promptly made copies of the *Pink* magazine profile of Ms. Steinem and made it mandatory reading for all of my team at Real Living. I don't have to tell you, of course, that Gloria Steinem founded NOW—the National Organization for Women—and *Ms.* magazine and led the second wave of feminism. You knew that, right? I asked a couple of my favorite 20-somethings their impressions upon seeing an amazing, empowered unstuck woman in action, and here is what they said:

Erin Corrigan: *Before hearing her speak, I was familiar with the name Gloria Steinem, but I wasn't exactly sure what her place in herstory was. Until recently, I had been fairly blind to the need for positive change for women, primarily for three reasons:*

1. *I had attended an all-girls high school, where we did it all, from sports to student government to Latin Club.*

2. *I'd studied a more progressive industry, graphic design, in college. Roughly half of the designers out there are women, unlike engineering or math, where we are a dramatic minority.*

3. *I'd been building my career in a work environment built by women.*

The date of her speaking engagement came at a time when I began noticing an influx of women—and some men— who were working to create positive change and new opportunities for women and girls. And not just because of the general needs that we see in statistics, but the benefits surrounding the energy and sisterhood that women experience when working toward a common goal. The fact that it's hard for some to see the need for change is a double-edged sword. Obviously, the progress we've made, thanks to Gloria and her supporters, thus far is incredible; but it does lead some to believe there isn't much left to be done.

Recently, a friend asked me if I was really a feminist— apparently I didn't fit his mental picture of one. I was so caught off-guard by the question that I couldn't find the right response at the time, but if the words had come, I would have said:

A feminist:

♦ *Believes women should earn as much as men for the same job*

♦ *Knows a woman can do anything a man can do*

♦ *Wants equal opportunities and rights for women everywhere*

So the question is not whether I am a feminist, but rather, why aren't you one?

Kelly Kinzer Malone: *Gloria Steinem was a name I barely remembered from a women's studies class I took in college. Gloria's coming to town opened many conversations about women's issues in our company—and in my household. Through these discussions, I changed my perspective on a few things. As a newlywed, I'm proud to say that I still use my maiden name, even though my husband was dead-set against it. He said I've only been a professional for two years, it's not important at this point. But it is important to me.*

To keep my identity. To keep what I've built. And to maintain my independence.

Also, I've realized the importance of empowering women—in my family and in the workplace. My boss does it daily, my mother did it throughout my childhood, and now it's my turn. Simple things that you don't realize greatly affect your team. Offering a team member a chance for a promotion. Letting another women know that she is doing a great job. Sending young women to conferences, and encouraging professional development and community involvement. In the hustle and bustle of the workday, take the time to let others know they're special, needed. Those are things I see in my company, and those are the things that make me happy I'm here. If every company was run this way, the future would be very bright.

Gloria is sparking conversations even today. I'm certain similar reactions were felt by every one of the women—and men—in the sold-out auditorium. When you're feeling stuck, think about how far you've come. How far we've come together. Take somebody to lunch who is part of your network but that you haven't seen in a while. Inspiration is all around you. You just have to tune in to it. Reach up, to women older than you. Reach down, to those younger.

The Real You within and in your business will benefit. Guaranteed.

A Real Story

Connie Leal Ballenger

Meet Connie Leal Ballenger, born in 1962, founder and owner of upscale fashion boutique, Leal. Business owner since 1993.

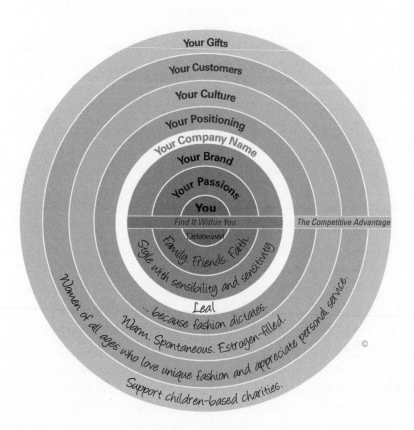

After college, I entered the world of public accounting, working at two large international accounting firms and a leading retail conglomerate. It was still the kind of environment that was new for women, so there really wasn't a culture of supporting other women. It was about survival and proving yourself.

I toiled away over the years, always thinking in the back of my mind that I wanted to do something else. Sometimes you need a push to do the right thing. For me, it came one particular year that I was on track for a major promotion. My performance reviews had been outstanding, my clients were happy, and my projects were running smoothly.

To make a long story short, I didn't get the promotion. I was told I was too soft and needed to work another year and get a little tougher. It was insulting after I had just landed a big job for the company. I decided then I needed to leave. But I wasn't going anywhere without the promotion. I wasn't going to give them a reason not to promote me again.

I stayed another year and received my promotion. Then I left to form my retail venture—Leal—my maiden name. I had always loved fashion and saw a void for a new type of upscale women's retailer. Sure, there were competitors selling similar fashions, but I wanted to take it to another level. When I designed the store, I installed a small kitchenette with an espresso machine in the back hidden by a decorative panel and easily accessible to a comfortable sitting area. My goal was to serve espresso and wine and create a gathering space for women whether they wanted to shop or not. From the start, the concept worked.

How well was really brought home to me after 9/11. People shut down, and I assumed that my business would suffer. But, just the opposite occurred. That September and October women congregated at my store to talk, to share. For them, it became a support place, a safe place to gather. It was comfortable, genuine, and made my store feel like an old-fashioned neighborhood hangout. I loved connecting with my clients (friends) that way. I think it's what has distinguished me from my competition, too. I've kept it small and personal, and my clients have responded.

I also saw my store as a way to help other women realize their own dreams, and that has transpired. Young, single women, moms who haven't been in the workforce for years, women who are searching for a career change—these women and many others have all worked here. And, I'm excited to report many of them have left and gone on to start their own businesses.

Connie could have stayed stuck at her big corporate job. But she didn't. She followed her dreams, creatively, and that's what you're doing, too. Her boutique is genuine, real, thoughtful—a direct reflection of her and her vision. And customers have responded and continued to respond. Retail ventures have one of the highest failure rates of all startups, yet she continues to thrive. You know why? She's continued to empower other women throughout her career. It's not just about her Real business. It's also about the gifts she shares with the women she touches. I bet she's glad she didn't get the promotion the first time around.

RECOMMENDED READING

♦ If you feel stuck, check out Elizabeth Gilbert's *Eat, Pray, Love: One Woman's Search for Everything Across Italy, India and Indonesia* for inspiration. And any profile, article, or the like by Gloria Steinem. It's worth it.

Life Lesson Twenty-Three: Play

I love to laugh. Sometimes people accuse me of laughing too much, and my middle son, firmly entrenched in middle school, doesn't allow me to laugh in front of his friends. I'll admit it, I have a honk/snort laugh. But laughter is important, even when embarassing. So is having fun and playing. Whatever that means to you.

Serendipity struck on a recent trip to New York. While wandering through SoHo on a beautiful summer Sunday, a pink banner drew my attention. It promoted the name of a favorite designer, Nanette Lepore. Now, I had presumed Nanette Lepore was a female designer—at least I hoped she wasn't a conglomerate posing as one—with hip, fun flair. Entering the boutique confirmed everything her clothing represents—fun, feminine, different—white floors, comfortable, and stylish. I asked the salesperson helping us about Nanette. Was she real? In fact, yes. Visit her web site, nanettelepore.com, for the rest of the story, but one of my favorite parts is that she is a woman entrepreneur from Youngstown, Ohio, a heartland heroine. And she's been in Manhattan designing since shortly after college. She's just like her clothes: savvy, feminine, sophisticated, cool. And real. Even her shopping bags—adorned with fat pink ribbons—are unique and stylish. She is what she is, in the design of a skirt, to the shopping bag and the web site. That's *Real You Incorporated* in action.

Talk about a business built with play in mind, and you have the best of all worlds. Build-A-Bear Workshops, those wonderful places where you watch your child build a customized teddy bear and insert a beating heart, was created by a woman entrepreneur by the name of Maxine Clark. Now, pantyhose are no fun and Sara Blakely, inventor of Spanx, agreed and changed the world—at least the women's lingerie world. Sara broadened her product offering, made millions, starred on a reality TV show, and most important, launched the Sara Blakely Foundation to help change the world for women and girls. What could be better? Bet Sara's smiling at work and happy in life. She's tapping into creativity, enjoying success, and giving back. If you're smiling at work, and at other women's successes, you too are tapping into that play element of life that we all need to survive. If not, start tapping right now.

Every budding entrepreneur needs inspiration. SARK (Susan Ariel Rainbow Kennedy), author of *Succulent Wild Woman: Dancing with your Wonder-full Self,* can get your creative process flowing and give you that sense of fun that sometimes slips away as we get overwhelmed by life, business, or home. Her books also force you into making your dreams real, something I hope this book has done as well. Remember, it's your world you're creating. You can have fun *and* be taken seriously. You can smile and laugh *and* be smart. Play will help you feel more alive. If you've lost it, bring it back into your life.

A wonderful entrepreneurial-spirited woman I know, Gloria Rau, recently told me she knows she's successful if she hears people laughing outside her office. That means the people in the office are having fun, relating, and growing together as a team. Work is hard enough, she says, without having an office environment where fun and joy is encouraged. I couldn't agree with her more completely.

Did you know preschool children laugh up to 400 times a day but by adulthood, we laugh only a measly 17 times a day, on average?

Let's change that, shall we? According to researchers at Loma Linda University School of Medicine, laughter reduces the level of stress hormones and stimulates the immune system. Laughter also provides a physical stress relief, is a good workout for your stomach, and connects us with others. Remember the scene in Mary Poppins as the laughing kids floated to the ceiling? The more they laughed, the higher they floated. There you have it. You know Mary was watching the children so their mother could attend the suffragettes protest, right?

Go have some fun.

A Real Story

Jane Arthur-Roslovic

Meet Jane Arthur-Roslovic, born in 1962. Principal,
The Kingswood Company, jewelry cleaner manufacturer,
founded in 1956. Business purchased by Jane and her
partner in 2005.

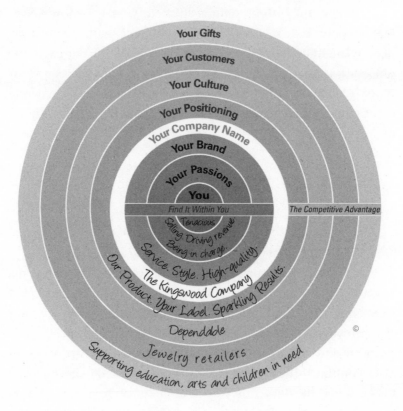

I love being an entrepreneur. I started my first company right out of college after completing a course on entrepreneurship. I fell in love with the company I created. Now, with my manufacturing business, it feels the same. Sure, there are many tough challenges. I used to agonize over the conflict between work and home, but now I know it's the best thing for my kids to see me as a happy, successful, working, entrepreneurial mom. My daughter and son have great lives. Because I own my company, I can be there for them when they need me. If I want to take the afternoon and go hang out with my kids, I do. Their lives are enriched because of my business, not the opposite. We spend quality time together and have fun. I think that's the key. I'm thrilled with my choices, and there is balance, if you stay true to yourself.

Work in and of itself is fun. I love the daily interaction with employees and customers on a professional and personal level. I thoroughly enjoy going to trade shows and meeting customers that I usually only communicate with over the phone. Getting to know people and how they think and react is really a huge part of my happiness. I relish the work involved in landing a large account as well as a small one. It pushes all of our teams— art department, logistics, customer service, and production—to provide a terrific product on time and at the right price! Once the order is shipped, the pride of the company is so great. The teamwork and effort that goes on during this process creates such a positive and uplifting experience for everyone involved. The fun is in accomplishing results and growing many rewarding relationships. People around you every day, whom you enjoy—that's what it's all about. I never imagined I'd be a jewelry cleaner manufacturer—and now I can't imagine my life without this business.

For fun, Jane goes to work. Or plays with her kids. Or both. The choice is hers. She is enjoying the life she's created, and it shows. Being happy and playful does not make her any less successful. In fact, it makes her more. Give it a shot.

♦ Anything by SARK, but especially fun are her Juicy Living cards. I have a set on my desk to keep me smiling at work. Today's card reads: "Your life is an adventure." I love that.

Life Lesson Twenty-four: Share

Perhaps sharing is a natural human tendency, but as women, we excel at it. I recently heard of an African word: *Ubuntu*. It means no human being is completely self-sufficient. We are all interdependent. It is also a phrase that describes communal harmony— the sense that revenge and anger destroy, while forgiveness and helping build. Ubuntu is why there are women entrepreneurs across the globe emerging and connecting to help one another through the power of the Internet.

A recent article in *The Times of India* boasted that: "Asian women are raking in more moolah than any other female entrepreneurs worldwide. Interestingly, while business is the main source of wealth for at least 26 percent of Asian women entrepreneurs, the global figure stands at 20 percent. Even more heartening is that Asian women are outperforming their sisters in developed nations and how! Whether it's Perween Warsi of Bihar, who is now better known as the Samosa queen of London, or an enterprising Kiran Mazumdar Shaw, who made a mark with her managerial skills in the corporate world, entrepreneurship seems to have its own share of Sunita Williamses and Angelina Jolies. The Chinese nu (woman) and Bharatiya nari come to share the common ground here as they draw wealth from entrepreneurship."

You are part of a global movement of female-driven entrepreneurialism. Women create community and change the world in ways big and small, every day.

At some point, there will be a female president of the
United States.

Hopefully soon. While there are arguments to be made on all sides of the political spectrum, the plain fact is that things would be different if the composition of the government reflected the composition of its constituents. It just would. And, as a woman, you know things would be better.

And while we are on the path to equality, don't forget your own personal support system to help your dreams stay on the right path. It's essential to practice asking for, and accepting, help and guidance. It's tough. I know, you're supposed to be superwoman. But allowing others to help you helps them in return. Thereby, practicing Ubuntu.

No homework here, just pure inspiration from one of the most spunkerific, empowered, and successful entrepreneurs I've encountered.

A Real Story

Judi Sheppard Missett

Meet Judi Sheppard Missett, born in 1944, president and CEO of Jazzercise, Inc., a dance fitness program. Business owner since age 11.

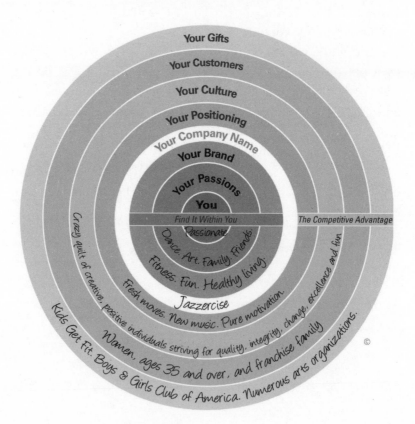

My passion is dance, and I've been doing it since age 11 when I opened my own dance studio in Red Oak, Iowa. After just a few months, I had nearly 100 students. At age 14, I started working professionally as a dancer. During college, I worked in theater to help my parents pay my tuition. After graduation, I continued performing in theater and modeling, as well as dancing with my friend and mentor, Gus Giordano. Gus is one of the most famous jazz dance masters in the world, and he helped me in my career path, giving me the room to grow as a dancer and teacher. In fact, it was Gus who encouraged me to stray from conventional teaching methods. In 1968, I had my first child, Shanna Suzanne. One year later, I gave birth to another "child"—Jazzercise.

There's a unique, rich corporate culture at Jazzercise, made up of a crazy quilt of creative, positive individuals. With all of our 150 corporate employees, we stress a work environment that is open to creativity and input. While we take our work seriously, we also take pride in our fun, casual, and friendly work environment. If you saw our company walking down the street, it would look like an abstract piece of art with lots of color, expression, and movement all woven into an attractive overall package that gives off great energy. That's who we are.

My daughter, Shanna, is executive vice president of Jazzercise. She is involved in many aspects of the company, and will keep the company moving forward. I also have two granddaughters who are 5 and 2, and I foresee both of them becoming involved in the company down the line. The older one, Skyla, already is quite a dancer.

I never had a blueprint or master plan to become an entrepreneurial business owner. I simply followed my passion. The business opportunity developed in front of me, so I literally took it and ran. I had no financial backing or formal business plan, but allowed my business to evolve by:

1. *Being passionate.*

2. *Allowing for change—the courage to change by listening to my gut and never fearing failure. As we grow, we reinvent ourselves.*

3. *Combining mind-body-spirit through surrounding yourself with people who lift you up, a family culture, and remembering to give back.*

In addition to her role as an entrepreneur, wife, mother, and grandmother, Judi is a great philanthropist, having raised more than $26 million for various charities. She gladly shares her story with women across the country.

In fact, part of Ubuntu is sharing your story. It helps you build your real brand, too. So share with your friends. With your sons and daughters. With us. Share your stories and your RYI chart with us online at realyouincorporated.com. You can also create and download your RYI chart in your favorite color scheme. Visit and see! You'll find more profiles, more inspiration, and links to many of the organizations referred to throughout the book. Send us your empowering stories. We'd love to include you in the next book! Join us, and let's see where we can go. Good luck as you share the Real You with the world. Welcome to the revolution.

> *"Like art, revolutions come from combining what exists into what has never existed before."*
> —Gloria Steinem

A Real Story

You

This is your *Real You Incorporated* chart. Fill it in
to create the tangible foundation for your dreams.

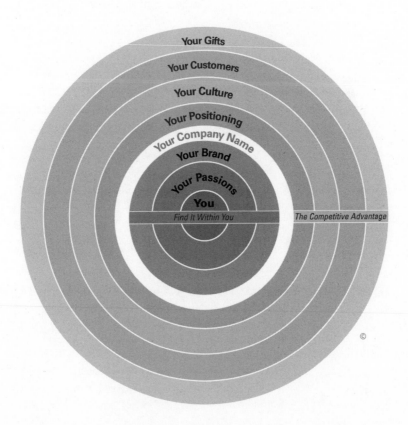

Acknowledgments

Okay, it's true. The people I want to thank are countless and endless, and no doubt I will omit many. Pardon me in advance, but know, the rest of the readers who don't know me hope this will be very brief, so I will give it a try.

I want to thank all of the inspiring women entrepreneurs I've met, who are in the book, on the web site or hopefully will be. Especially inspiring are the agents and broker-owners of the Real Living network. The managers of our offices, as well as the seasoned professionals, help budding entrepreneurs make their dreams come true. I'm especially thankful to Linda Altomare, Gloria Rau, and Sara Walsh for their support and leadership examples. Thank you all for inspiring *Real You Incorporated*—putting the entrepreneurial spirit into action as you help people with their dreams of home ownership while building your own dream businesses.

Thanks, too, to my team at the Real Living corporate office in Columbus, in the heart of Ohio, in the heart of America. When it came time to rally around this book, and get it out the door, some folks were especially adept at picking up my slack. Thanks to Sarah Shoemaker, Bill Evans, Caroline Shroyer, Gretchen Bartholomew, Chris Svec, Bob McAdams, and Craig Hauzie who held down the fort as the rest of our team was deputized to get this book finished. Especially so, my brilliant creative director, Erin Corrigan, who designed the cover and most of the art inside of *Real You Incorporated* and to Alex Green, my Radar, who attempted to bring order to chaos and always does it with style. To the rest of the marketing team, thank you, Mike Maxwell, Emilie Smith, Dina Temkin, and David Cifoni. Thanks also to Traci

Crabtree and Brandy Brown who jumped in to help with enthusiasm and creativity, whenever asked.

As I always say, it takes a village to raise a Rouda, to borrow from the Hillary Clinton book. When someone asks how do you do it, I thank my village. While I'm working, I know my kids are happy and taken care of thanks to women such as Kristen Adams, Lisa Young, and Olivia Ost, amazing women who create a team that makes it okay to be a working mom. Thanks, too, to our family—Harley and Marlese Rouda and Pat Sturdivant—key village people.

To Sarah Mills Bacha, a special friend, who helped me get organized and get going on this project, and to Kathleen Murphy, a wonderful friend and mentor, who helped shepherd it along. To Sharon Steele and Cindy Lazarus, inspiring women both with a passion to help other women achieve.

Girlfriends, to me, are family. And with this project, I needed all the encouragement I could get! Thanks to Cathy Walker, Elizabeth Paulsen, Kathleen Cottingham, Jane Arthur-Roslovic, Meg Melvin, Melissa Wallace, Connie Ballenger, Trish Cadwallader, Maureen Miller, Jackie Cassara, Colleen Kennedy Sturdivant (family and friend) and Beth Dinsmore for encouraging me with this project, and many others along the way. My life is richer because you're in it.

Also on the editorial side, I'd like to thank the only boss I've been able to keep, Ben Cason—editor of my newspaper column—who helped edit and improve this work. To Doral Chenoweth, Keith Schneider, and Keith Ferrazzi, each for different reasons and you each know why. To David Ratner, a remarkable book publicist and friend, who somehow helped me find my wonderful agent, Helen Rees, even though neither of us knew how things were supposed to work. And to Helen who found Laurie Harting, my fabulous senior editor at Wiley, and Shannon Vargo, another fabulous Wiley editor. It really is a thrill to work with her and her team of Kate Lindsay and Jessica Langan-Peck. I've learned so much and grown as a writer by knowing you all.

A very special thank you to Kelly Kinzer Malone, who has been the behind-the-scenes editor, confidante, ego booster, and all-around amazing young woman. Thank you, Kelly. For everything. This book would not be here without you. When the going gets tough, the real people in your life step forward. That's you.

To my amazing kids, the loves of my life. My boys—Trace, Shea, and Dylan—who are growing into confident, enterprising, and empowering young men. I am so proud of each of them. And thankful they—for the most part—put up with a very nontraditional mom, who has taught them to spy sexism and stop it. And to my daughter, Avery, who is, without doubt, at the heart of my hopes for the next generation. She will lead the way with her smile, her energy, and her quiet power. I can't wait to watch her become.

And finally, to my husband, Harley. What would I do without you? You are the essence of roots and wings: providing me with the encouragement to achieve, while keeping me anchored at home. My friend. My business partner. All my life. All my love.

Enough about me. I hope you've discovered the Real You and enjoyed this book. Visit realyouincorporated.com to share your thoughts and find more inspiration.

All the best,
Kaira Sturdivant Rouda

About the Author

Kaira Sturdivant Rouda, currently president of Real Living and creator of the Real Living brand, is passionate about entrepreneurialism, marketing, and the power of women in the workforce and beyond. A published author, writer, marketing executive, and business owner, she built her career by working in marketing for national brands, large regional advertising agencies, and national and regional publications.

While maintaining her own writing business, Kaira became the vice president of marketing for an *Inc.* 100 national franchisor, where she found her passion for franchising as a means to entrepreneurial business ownership. In 1997, she entered another field filled with entrepreneurs—residential real estate. In 2002, she launched the nationally award-winning Real Living brand, now among the fastest growing franchise companies in the country and making a dramatic impact in an industry in flux.

Active in her community, Kaira founded Central Ohio's first homeless shelter for families, served two terms on the board of the Mid-Ohio FoodBank, and now serves on the board of the YWCA and is an underwriter of The Women's Fund. She has received numerous awards for her civic service, including the Ohio Sertoma Service to Mankind Award, Kiwanis Humanitarian Award, and Northwest Rotary Woman of the Year. Kaira was recognized by *Entrepreneur* magazine as heading one of the 50 Fastest-Growing Women-Led Businesses with Real Living.

A member of the Women Presidents' Organization, the Google Real Estate Advisory Board, and a WebAward judge for the Web

Marketing Association, Kaira is a nationally recognized speaker and continues to write a newspaper column and fiction books. A magna cum laude graduate of Vanderbilt University, she and her husband live in Columbus, Ohio, with their four children. For more, visit www.realyouincorporated.com.

Index